MOUNTAIN TIME

*Also by Jane Candia Coleman
in Large Print:*

Doc Holliday's Gone
I, Pearl Hart
The O'Keefe Empire
Borderlands

This Large Print Book carries the
Seal of Approval of N.A.V.H.

MOUNTAIN TIME

A Western Memoir

Jane Candia Coleman

Thorndike Press • Waterville, Maine

Published in 2002 by arrangement with
Golden West Literary Agency.

Thorndike Press Large Print Western Series.

The tree indicium is a trademark of Thorndike Press.

The text of this Large Print edition is unabridged.
Other aspects of the book may vary from the original edition.

Set in 16 pt. Plantin by Al Chase.

Printed in the United States on permanent paper.

Library of Congress Cataloging-in-Publication Data

Coleman, Jane Candia.
    Mountain time : a western memoir / Jane Candia Coleman.
      p. cm.
    Originally published: Waterville, Me.:Five Star, 2001, in series: Five Star first edition western series.
    ISBN 0-7862-2734-6 (lg. print : hc : alk. paper)
    1. Coleman, Jane Candia — Homes and haunts — West (U.S.) 2. Authors, American — 20th century — Biography. 3. West (U.S.) — Social life and customs. 4. West (U.S.) — Description and travel. 5. Western stories — Authorship. 6. Large type books. I. Title.
PS3553.O47427 Z466 2002
813'.54—dc21
  [B]   2002019917

MOUNTAIN TIME

Prologue

Light

This week I have driven hundreds of miles from the great southeastern valleys of Arizona to the Gila Mountains of New Mexico, and in every one of those miles was another seeing.

If it is possible to exhaust the visual memory, I have done so. Inside I am heavy and weightless both at once. I draw memories out one by one and together, for they run together, a melting pot of emotion.

It is always the light that astounds, the light of a thousand miles of sky reflected, absorbed by the palette of pale earth. Beside this Southwestern light, Arles fades, and Venice, the Côte d'Azur, and the single-rayed luminosities of Rembrandt. Both daunting and poignant, it sears through the eyes and into the heart where it becomes a part of the body's pulse, a memory felt when no longer seen.

And the light of late fall is most miraculous of all, burning, lifting, singing, a tangible, musical thing that quivers and strikes where and when it will.

I have seen so much light, so much violent color, so many fires, that my mind is exhausted with the recording of it. I am touched with ocher, rose, shimmering gold, with the silver of the moon, the flanks of stone mountains washed with a shade of apricot so unreal no painter would dare attempt reproduction.

Whoever first named New Mexico "The Land of Enchantment" was blessed with vision and with a sense of fantasy. Cross the border between the states, and you are, indeed, enchanted, more so the farther you go.

Route I-10 leads through Stein's Pass, a jumble of golden mountains, and down onto the Animas Playa. In summer this stretch of white sand is blinding. It reflects the heat, the light with the intensity of a furnace, a parched, drifting desert of alkali. In fall it fills with water from the rains, becomes an unbounded sheet of blue broken by stems of grass, by the lifting off of water birds. It is more mirage than actuality, especially for one who has known it in July. If I were to walk toward it, would it recede, lure me into the vast anatomy of the plain? Would the birds rise, startled and clucking at my approach? Would the whistling swan unfold, a true mirage, or geese lift, honking their winter music? I do not go. Perhaps there is in me a place that prefers fantasy to reality, that does not wish to put imagination to the test for fear of damaging what is enchanted.

At Lordsburg we turn off for Silver City. The road rises up a long hill, gradually but steadily. Behind us the Playa shimmers, the mountain ranges fade out in successive lines of blue and lavender, one of the few abstractions in nature, a challenge to the eyes and fingers of the artist. Who among us could mix or even visualize the myriad tones, depths, shades of blue? Water, hills, mountains, cañons repeating one after the other until the sky, itself a pale and shimmering blue unlike any other.

"It's all too much," I say, as I say often. Looking down, I see my hands balled into fists, symbols of the futility of possessing any part of what I see. "I wish I were immortal."

"Why?" my friend asks.

And I say: "So I could stand here forever and see, and nothing would ever change. Then I'd have a chance at it."

But how to choose the time and place for one's immortality? As we move ahead, the sun drops behind us, breathes fire at earth and sky. The road is lined with chamiso blooming. The golden flower heads, the grayish foliage, deepen in color and toss in the wind, searing me with intensity — theirs and my own response. And the land ahead begins to burn, the flanks and shoulders of the mountains turning rose, then crimson, an impossible radiance that lingers even when the sun has gone. In the Swiss Alps this phenomenon is labeled "Alpenglow," a word that, like most, fails to capture the actuality or the response. What was earth, rock, crevice is now only a softness, coals dwindling beneath the ashes of the slow dark — a promise of warmth, the gentle tongue of land unchanged, unchanging.

In Silver City the air is clean, the smell of piñon fires a drug. I walk, nose in the air like a dog, tasting it all, and finally sink down in sleep with the colors and shapes of earth whirling behind my eyes like the pattern of a quilt.

In the morning there is frost. The junipers sparkle, and the long russet grasses of autumn. Along the creeks and bottoms, cottonwoods and poplars dance their ceaseless yellow dance against the sky — ilk flags, golden shoes, small faces lifting and falling with or without wind, as if, in the fastening of leaf to twig, there is electricity, a spark that lights and stimulates.

You cannot look at them for long, but must turn away, fasten on the mundane myself, for here it is still autumn; the chamiso sways, trees burst from the river bottom luminous as fireworks, and ristras, those strings of red chilies so vital to Southwesterners, gleam on every farm wall, every porch.

The land changes from desert to pasture to rolling prairie covered with red furze like the hide of an animal. The rise and fall are a shape somehow female, like the curves of my own body, so that, looking, I see myself magnified, stretching over the plain. Perhaps it is this similarity that gave rise to myth, to the ancient belief that earth is woman, that in winter she sleeps, holding life within.

The swell of the land, the dried stalks of reeds goad me to thought. To write what I must write, what I am driven to do, I must labor as with child. I must walk this land, touch, taste, smell. I must look inward, digging deep, and outward, as far as the sky. My hands will learn the shapes of stems, the weight of rock, the feather touch of prairie grass. I will root into memory, intellect, imagination, into self, and into the depths of earth to find what is necessary.

I stare at sky, at clouds that are the shape and color of winter, at the cold shoulders of mountains. The Aldo Leopold Wilderness falls away at my feet, and I lean toward it, hungering.

"I've lost you," my friend says.

"No," I answer. "I think I've just been found." And so it is. This is the Enchanted Land and it has touched me — today, tomorrow, and forever.

If there is a constant in life, it is the fact of change. Nothing, not tree, bird, grain of sand, remains immobile or untouched by its surroundings. My wish for immortality was an idle one, a momentary desire that, given the context of these two days, becomes a denial of life, not a confirmation. I am not the woman I was, nor the girl. I am different from what I was this morning, yesterday, five miles ago. Change is the way of things, part of the natural order. Nothing remains the same, and there is a happiness in newness of place, circumstance, ability. There is a challenge, and in that challenge lies the reason for life.

I awake to snow. The whiteness blinds, and the reflection of the sun. There is snow, and there are tracks upon it: the triangular markings of doves, the soft leapings of rabbits, the tracks of dogs like winter flowers. Junipers bend down, great filigree balls that rest, quiver, leap up as the snow slips off. Each stalk of grass has a covering of ice. In the river bottoms the poplars are dancing unchanged. If anything, they are more beautiful, their gold singing against the purity.

I walk, touch the blue shadows, the weighted stalks. The air is the cold of the mountains, proof of clouds. The sentinel ravens caw as I move. Black, their wings make blacker shadows across the shining. I reach out and catch the shadows in my hands.

The Night Song of the Porcupine

November

In the middle of a still, moonlit night, I wake myself singing.

At first I am sure that the song that flows around me like my life — sorrowful, ruminative, with moments of joy and infinite clarity — is music from my own heart.

And then, listening, comes the realization that I am not the singer, that someone speaks for me, and the fact is bitter, for who dares tell my feelings, who knows me so well that they can?

I am now wide awake, afraid to move for fear of shattering a solitude so deep it has no starting point, no end, a wilderness of rivers, grass, mountains touching night with cold stone mouths. I lie hardly breathing, foolishly attempting to give a name to what I hear and thus to possess the source.

Monks in medieval cloisters could have sung this minor scale so different from our modern one, and in that difference so much closer to the rhythms of earth. Monks making prayerful perambulations through gardens of herbs, compline and the Angelus trailing the small paths in their wake.

Through the open door come moonlight and the scent of crushed sage as if, indeed, someone has stood outside a moment, lost in musing. And then the monk song dwindles, is replaced by the plucked notes of a samisen, again a different scale, like water falling, one drop, then another, like a road winding away. It is a very long road. I know. I have followed it from its beginning, across prairie and the first thrust of young mountains to this place where music and moon intertwine.

How long I lie thus, motionless, I cannot tell, but when the song fades into distance, I am bereft, graceless, a human form silent in a bed where minutes before I had been blessed with wings.

Who sang?

What?

In the morning I ask myself. It was not a dream. It was the voice of a solitary wanderer telling a history, amusing itself in the vastness of night, calling for response from creatures similar to itself.

What I heard was the spinning out of knowledge I could no longer understand, but which the web of my body shared. In us all there is a reservoir of memory, a community of experience, even with the smallest, and in my pavilion of moonlight an ancient well was revealed to me, and with it my own reflection.

Words from a book read in childhood come back to me from that well, as if I knew they would be needed and stored them there . . . "The rare song of the porcupine. . . ." The book is forgotten; the truth retained.

Now I look back at my life and wonder where my odyssey began. I remember a small child gazing in awe at the colors of mesa and sky on a movie screen, devouring whole libraries of books on travel, wildlife, mustangs, rifles, Indians, and history, books in which girl-children were supposed to have no interest. I remember walking through woods and listening to the trees, running wild as any mustang and tasting the wind. My hunger was there from the beginning, and, when I finally touched the bones of earth and marveled at their unconcerned nakedness, when I stood and watched prairie reaching to sky, I was moved as by nothing else until last night's music awakened me. I loved, and that love obliterated all barriers between me and what I recognized as home.

Memories come back like flickers of night song. People, places, spoken words both harsh and gentle, the colors of things, all unfold and drift in that place behind my eyes where imagination surfaces as shadows to be given shape by discipline. . . .

The Chiricahua Mountains dominate Arizona's southeast corner. Running north-south, they form a natural and nearly impenetrable barrier between Arizona and New Mexico, their red rhyolite skeleton carved into cañons, cliffs, and towering rock figures. Only the strong survive here, those who can summon fortitude, who can "make do." It is no accident that these mountains were the home and the last retreat of the Chiricahua Apaches — of Cochise and the iron-jawed Geronimo — whose faces could have been hewn from the rocks they fought from, who were the last of the American Indians to surrender, who fought on foot, on horseback, and like mirages in the desert out of hatred and out of love.

Faces like theirs are still in evidence, both red and white. These mountains leave their mark, brand the souls and shape the bones of those who live in them. And this is no mystery, for the land molds us to our destiny, good or bad. In the final analysis it is how man exists with his environment that makes him what he is — rancher, banker, outlaw.

And women? What of them? I can speak only with knowledge of the survivors, those who lived through loneliness and drought, who grew up without even the simplest conveniences but whose eyes still dance, whose shoulders are sturdy. These women cherish the dawns and the sunsets, the turtles and the deer, the plants, both cultivated and indigenous, and find in all a sense of wonder.

I can speak only for myself, product of the East yet yearning from first memory for this place of space and winds. I remember the first time I came here, to a ranch, in winter. I felt like a wheel rolling along the red dust track between dried chamiso, the yellow, brittle globes of horse nettle, and tumbleweed. It was twilight when I came to the Sulphur Springs Valley. A moon, nearly full, hung over Chiricahua Peak, although the western sky still burned, the purple of plums.

As if drawn by a magnet I crossed the valley, went up the narrow road toward Turkey Creek. It was not so many years ago, but lifetimes may be lived in seconds, and time, the time named by the mind, is not always relevant.

I came as a tenderfoot, as green as any wife of a hundred years before, as innocent of struggle with earth. And then the mountains spoke. Some shadow or coyote's howling cried out and was understood, and I began to change, imperceptibly at first. I went East and found that what had been familiar was ridiculous and sometimes frightening. Skyscrapers threatened. Who were all those people? Cities cut off breath. Feminine niceties seemed foolish. My acquiescence to marital abuse began to chafe. I was becoming a person and seeing myself as one. The red rock of the mountains was in me, and the honesty, for the land is honest. Mountains cannot hide themselves. The rain does not lie, nor the drought.

I knew nothing else. Not the names of growing things or the truth of history. So I set out to learn the people, the mysteries with the unwitting help of an old man, Archie, grandson of pioneer settlers.

Year in and year out we sat, sometimes in his blue trailer, sometimes over supper in my kitchen at the ranch. And we talked while the afternoon burned away over the flats, while the moon rose and owls hooted their own stories in the trees.

And we forged a bond, the old man and I. A bond of love.

The place where it began was called, then, Sunglow Ranch. The mountains turned crimson in the twilight there, and the months of summer shimmered in the sun. Every year I returned to it with my family: to its people, its horses, its clear beauty high in the mountains I loved above all others. It was the place that, for six years and in the absence of another, I called "home."

Part One

Shadows in My Hands
1979–1986

The Chiricahua Mountains

The Ranch

Woodie comes to the airport, and at the sight of his lean, weathered face I am filled with joy. He himself is a joyous person. He radiates happiness. He loves people, life, animals, the ranch that is his home, and daily thanks God for all of them.

He says that Archie is ailing. I thought he was well again after a stay in a Tucson hospital. Tomorrow I will walk the washed-out road to see him.

This year it is green in the high valleys. There has been a lot of rain. The grass is high, and it is the season of sunflowers. They line the road, their leaves a darker green than any other, their flowers tossing as we pass.

Down, across a wash, up a grade, and there, suddenly, is the ranch: low white buildings around a courtyard, the original, tin-roofed ranch house, tack room, and corrals off to one side. And beyond them all, the mountains, the southern end of the Chiricahuas, immovable, enduring. It is the hour when they reflect the setting sun. They

27

seem to float just above the ground, to burn with a fierce flame. Amidst the bustle of arrival I stand and look at them. They have not changed in a year, perhaps not in a thousand.

There is something I must learn from them. I look and look, imprint them on the film of memory. They will be there tomorrow and the day after, but never again will they look the same as now, like golden lions stretching their paws.

"Mountains," I say to myself. "Chiricahua Mountains." I do not know why I say it, but there is a place within that responds, that closes around the sounds.

Jeanne runs across the field, ducking around the clothes poles. She is a small, spare, beautiful woman who has suffered illness, survived, and now makes a life here where, she says, although she is often alone she is never lonely. I have missed her during the past year, missed our long talks, our all-day shopping trips into Douglas seventy miles away. We hug each other as if we will never let go. It is her husband Al's birthday. "Come over for coffee and cake," she says, beaming. "Oh, it's good to see you!"

Last year we also arrived on Al's birthday. Archie came up then, and we sat telling tales, talking about the legend of the outlaw

28

John Ringo who is buried just up the road at the edge of Turkey Creek.

"My dad never believed he killed himself," Archie said. "He always said he was shot somewhere else, and whoever did it stuck him in that tree." It is an old riddle, the death of John Ringo, found bootless, horseless in the branches of a live oak, a bullet through his head.

We pondered the mystery in silence, then Archie told about a place in the mountains where an underground stream surfaces beneath the twisted roots of an old juniper tree. Huge trout swim there, and it is possible to catch them with bare hands because they are blind from swimming in the dark.

And then he told about the mountaintop where, each August, the ladybugs swarm. So many that the ground, the trees are obliterated and shine red. "Don't know whether they come to mate or whether they're just hatched," he said, his eyes far off as if he were envisioning the sight, "but it sure is something to see."

Last year he came up often, stayed to dinner, and, after I had cleared away the dishes, he would talk for hours about his life, the old ways, about animals and outlaws, grass and the drought, on and on in his low and musical voice, and we all sat silent and swaying under the lamplight. He is a storyteller as we do not know them any more, relic of a time when such an entertainment was an art. He weaves a spell, casts it upon his listeners, and all year I have been looking forward to more magic.

Change is often sad. Al has had a heart attack. He is still the same handsome, vigorous-looking man, but he is no longer allowed to ride. Riding was a great part of his life. In the past four years we have explored this whole part of the world with him, have learned the trails, gone to the silent places no one sees.

Tonight we talk about Captain, the new colt. He and his dam, Lassie, are down at Archie's. Tomorrow I shall see him. I will wake up to mountains, the sweetness of wind, ride my old companion, the sorrel gelding Laddie, see old friends.

I fall into bed and cannot sleep. I hear coyotes howling, owls down by the wash, crickets in the grass. The ranch cat runs across the roof. I get up, prowl, look out a long time. The mountains stand against sky, black on black. The moon has gone down. There is a stirring in me, an intuition of things too faint to grasp. What will come, will come. I return to bed and, this time, sleep.

★ ★ ★

I am awake at seven. I have hardly slept at all, but I don't care. I run barefoot for the sliding door to watch the mountains cast off night, purple-shadowed, stretching themselves.

Breakfast is quick, as it never is at home. We throw on jeans and boots and rush out to see the tank that is brimming with water, to the back trap to find the horses: Laddie, Chico, Duke, King, Prince. When I call, Laddie comes, shoves his soft nose into my chest. He remembers, I think. We have ridden together for four summers and have come to respect one another.

Woodie rides with us today, swinging up on Duke's tall back as if he is seventeen instead of seventy. We head west toward the rocky hills, toward Archie's. I am impatient. I have missed the old man.

Once through his tightly locked gate, we see Lassie and the colt making their way toward us through the weeds and tall grass. We ride quickly toward the corral, not knowing how the mare, a feisty creature, will react to strange horses.

Archie comes to the door, gaunt and hardly able to walk. Where has he gone, my sturdy old friend who could heft propane tanks, climb windmills, drive tractors and

31

trucks, and then sit talking for hours?

The fields dance around me. I am smitten with the fragility of all things. We are mortal. Earth and its time are finite. Yet his hand has the same warmth, his voice the old music. We smile at each other. Once again, I have found a Muse. In odd guise to be sure, but Muse he is. I have had Muses before. The shock of recognition, the unspoken flowing of language, is always the same. I no longer question it. It is a part of my life that I cannot explain, a precious gift. Muses come, and through them we see and love the world.

But today we have no time to talk. Without warning, Chico lies down in the corral and almost breaks his saddle. Prince, young and unsure, takes fright, hauls back, and breaks a rein.

"Having an ignorant fit," Archie says on his way to repair the broken leather. He is expert at making do. He has spent a lifetime "figuring," and has survived on that expertise for seventy years.

Now the colt comes to the fence. He pushes his head at me, gently, eyes filled with wonder. "Who are you?" he seems to be saying. "Who?" His breath is warm on my hand, his muzzle like satin. Whiskers tickle. I talk to him, making more sound than sense, and his ears follow my voice. He has deep, liquid eyes, and I see myself in them as on a convex mirror. Again I feel fragments of life, splintered images, and under them a dark and constant flowing, a stream of time, lives, existences. Colt, woman, the echo of an ancient joy, a mythic struggle between light and dark, male and female. Almost I know something. Almost I hear. Then the colt whirls and runs, scattering sunflowers and seed heads of grama grass. I am not sure if my intensity has frightened him or if he runs, like most young things, for the pleasure of moving, kicking up his heels, and bouncing, light as a thistle.

I call for Laddie, and he comes, ears pricked up, eyes gleaming.

"That little horse knows you," Archie says. "I thought last year you'd steal him for sure."

It is my joke. That some night I will ride up into the folds of the mountains with Laddie, and we will vanish as if we never were. If I did it, Archie would approve, would sit in his house chuckling because I got away with something.

On the way home we meet Don Jones on his lovely buckskin mare, Cinco. He's driven up for the weekend to round up cattle. "I could use some help," he says, looking at me.

I don't wait for permission. "I'll be there," I tell him.

Again I can't sleep. I stay awake, fearing I will miss the alarm, worrying about Archie down the road, ailing and stubborn. "I won't let you die," I say, as if I can keep him alive by force of will.

Coyotes are out again, a mixed chorus. They chuckle and wail as if they are being dismembered. I get up, peer out looking for them, see only dark shapes upon darkness. Trees. The old house. Mountains asleep.

The alarm goes off at five-thirty. The sky is gray, the color of shells. The moon rides over the corral. Tallow, grama grass, daisies are dew-soaked. They slap at my boots as I walk toward the tack house. The horses are there, yawning and looking at us with indignation. It's too early, they are saying. Where are we going this early?

An owl in a tree somewhere down by the wash is still hooting. The thrasher, mocking all, moves from one song to the next without pause. Mexican jays surge out ahead of us, giving alarm. Nothing moves unnoticed by them.

We pick up Don at his gate, split up after

34

agreeing to meet by the seep. Woodie and I head northwest. He leaves Laddie and me to climb the stony mountain while he rides the washes and draws.

We pick our way slowly. This is a rough climb over rocks, rolling stones, fallen century plants. Often the way is barred by the thorny branches of mesquite, too thick for us to go through. Laddie, used to the company of the other horses, is nervous at first, but I talk to him, keep up a constant flow of words. His ears twitch back and forth, and gradually he settles to the climb. We do it zigzagging. This is the first time we've been out alone to pick our own trail. It isn't easy. I must keep my eyes not only on the ground but all around us as well. I am, after all, looking for cattle. I begin to sing. Laddie curves his neck around, looks at me, then swings with the beat of "Sweet Betsy From Pike."

At the top of the hill we rest. I look straight across the Sulphur Springs Valley to the Dragoon Mountains. Cochise's stronghold, jumble of rocks, maze of cañons, burying place of the famous Apache chief, shows up purple in the early light. I can see a hundred miles. But I see no cattle, only Woodie, riding along at a fast walk below.

Directly ahead I hear a cow bawling, so Laddie and I begin our descent, finding the faint ruts of an old jeep trail. We follow the slope, cut around to the draw where I heard the cow. Rocks, dust, small wash with a little water, fresh cow dung, but no animals. Silence, Laddie's breathing, the hum of wind, and Woodie, riding along singing. Laddie and I follow the wash a way, cross it, ride down a small hump of stones. Eight o'clock and already hot, dry. Dust rises and whirls ahead of us. There is good grass by the wash and pools of dark water. We go on down to the seep but find nothing and climb up to the wide, rocky flat. The others have bunched their herd out on the road.

Nothing glamorous here. Cattle stink and draw flies. They are noisy and incredibly stupid. They kick up a cloud of dust that we in the rear inhale and swallow. "Come on, mamma! *Yup! Yup! Ho!*" Laddie has never worked cattle before, but it is in his blood. He is intelligent and takes to it quickly, ears working back and forth, nose at the broad rumps of the cows. He is by nature a dominant animal, and now, in this pushing of cattle, that dominance comes to the fore. He is in his element. He whirls on small hoofs as a calf breaks away, and pushes it back into the group. I am not sure whether I gave him a signal or whether, simultaneously, we gave chase.

We pen the herd, take a head count, and Don separates four steers belonging to someone else. He is working the cattle on foot, shouting and waving his rope. "Now I'm cuttin' cattle!" he yells, grinning.

We release the herd in a lower pasture until next week when the real roundup will begin.

Bad Medicine

The horses are turned out this morning for a well-deserved rest. I walk the mile to Archie's. I can walk this road in my sleep, rocks, gullies, and all. To my left is a broad pasture, very green and dotted with oak, juniper, Don's cows and calves. Behind this the great umber flanks of the mountains. To my right, a stony hill. Plains zinnias blaze out from crevices in the rock. Thistle poppies flutter white petals in the constant wind. The stalks of dead agave crown the hill, straight as utility poles. Behind this hill the seep where we rode yesterday, or, as Archie puts it, where I "played cowboy." In his eyes, one morning herding cattle can't take the dude out of me. He is right, but I feel as if I have done something and done it well. Next Saturday we will do it again. We'll round up, inoculate, cut horns, brand, castrate. We'll see who's playing cowboy.

I find him lying down on his brown couch, too weak to move. He is out of insulin and unable to drive the seventy miles to town. I say, hesitantly, that I will go to town if he trusts me to drive his truck. But he doesn't want to put me out. He hates dependency. He's never asked for anything in the whole of his life, has lived here alone with his mule, his mare, his red game hen, his cats, with his windmill for electricity, the mountains and his own thoughts for company; and he has never been beholden, just as none of his folks were ever beholden. But he's beaten now by his own body, as we are all beaten in the end. He'll go with me, he says. Just give him time to clean up.

I run back, make a quick lunch for my husband and the boys, explain to Jeanne what I'm doing. I tie a scarf, Indian-style, around my forehead. I hate hair blowing in my eyes when I drive. And, God help me, I have to drive well. If I strip the gears, run off the road, take a corner too close, I'll have dropped in Archie's regard. I know this, just as I know he is curious to see how this city woman will manage a truck.

His blue eyes are twinkling as he hands me into the cab. Once again comes the feeling that he's urging me on, giving me room. We grin at each other, and I move off. The gears are about two feet apart, third being halfway across the cab and reverse somewhere in the center of Archie's stomach as he sits ready to grab the wheel should disaster strike. One slip and it will be all over the county by next week. I know this in my soul, just as I know I have waited all my life to drive a truck. Where a woman brought up as I was gets such urges — horse stealing, riding roundup, driving trucks — I can't fathom, but they are there, have always been there.

"She pulls to the right a bit," he cautions as I head for the first cattle guard. "The tires are old."

"She feels fine." I have to concentrate. He has explained that he doesn't start off in first gear like everyone else, but in second, so I have to ease out the clutch, listen to the motor.

The big metal creature responds. It's fun! I relax, and he, knowing it, offers me a Camel from his ever-present pack. I've never smoked a Camel. Never driven any-thing this high, this big, this powerful. The feel of it is exciting. It is like driving a team, holding pure energy in my fingers.

Wind comes in at our faces, and dust. I straighten my headband; he adjusts the vent, courteous to the core. "You're doin' fine," he says, blowing a cloud of smoke.

I'm wild with it. With joy, pain, motion, power. With my own ability to handle a monster, with the sad reason for having to

40

do so. With pleasure at having found someone who knows me for what I am and neither approves nor disapproves but says: "Go it."

My own mother wouldn't recognize me now, or my husband, my friends. I am someone else. *Old man,* I think, *old man, this is not enough to do for you.*

But he has closed his eyes, rests his head on the back of the seat. His trust is my reward.

The town of Douglas has always felt like home. I am easy in it, the wide streets built in the days of cattle herds, the stores filled with cattlemen and Mexicans, the old-fashioned Gadsden Hotel with its cool marble lobby and overpowering stained glass. I am glad to be there again, glad I can find my way to the supermarket while Arch goes to the drugstore. I have Jeanne's shopping list and my own. Living seventy miles from a store has disadvantages. No one ever goes to town without assorted lists, without phoning the neighbors.

When we meet again, we sit a while in the truck, the doors open to catch the breeze, our legs stretched out. We smoke our Camels comfortably.

Since Arch was hospitalized in June, frightened by doctors who gave no thought to him as a human and certainly never took the time to realize the character or temperament of this particular patient, he has refused to speak of doctors even though he has an aneurysm that might kill him, diabetes, and several other debilitating ailments. I see he is worn out, white-faced under his sunburned skin. I let him tell me about "those doctors."

"I wasn't even a person to them," he says. "I was just a kind of guinea pig. I never even saw the head doctor, just a bunch of interns . . . youngsters. They said I'd be dead in a week."

"Well, you're not."

"Might as well be. Can't do anything any more."

My resolution grows. I'll get him to a doctor if I have to rope and drag him. "Think," I say. "There must be a doctor somewhere you like."

He sets his chin. "Most of them are dead," he says. "I used to know some Indians who really knew how to doctor. And without all those fancy machines to do it for them."

I should have expected that answer. For him the old ways are the only ways. Cat-scanners, X-rays, and all the rest have taken his dignity from him. How do I argue? How

42

persuade? I don't believe much in doctors myself, but I can't let this old man die out of stubbornness, alone and frightened. And he is frightened. "Those doctors" did a job on him from which he may not recover simply by the power of their suggestion. He has always been stronger, tougher than anyone. Now he faces his own mortality.

Does it happen to all of us? Do we all wind down our lives numbed and in terror? Will it happen to me? Will I die filled with pain and regret for the things that I lost or never found?

I look at him. Whatever the link between us, it is still firmly there.

"Those machines do save lives. We might not like them, but they work. And there are good doctors. There must be some around here. Think, Arch."

I want to touch him. To pour strength into him. In this moment I believe in the laying on of hands. But if I touch him, he will break and scatter like Captain at a sudden gesture.

He offers me another cigarette, strikes a match. I put my hands around his old leathery ones and keep them there.

"Think," I say again. We look squarely at one another.

"There is one," he says finally. "Fixed up

43

Mary pretty good."

"Where is he?"

"Here. In town."

"Well, then. I'll take you."

"He's bound to be busy. Might not have time."

If he doesn't have time, make time, I'll break his neck. "Does Al know him?"

A nod. "He went there with me before. For my nose."

Bless Al. Bless God. "He can make you an appointment."

"I guess." Bested, he puts his face in his hands and sighs. No, not bested. Worn out. Otherwise, I wouldn't have gotten around him so quickly.

On the way home he recovers enough to tell me that I drive like a city driver, gunning the engine at the take-off. But he says it with a twinkle. It is his way of giving praise. Praising anyone is difficult for him, but at least he does not say that I've been "playing truck driver."

I do not sleep much again, although wrung dry from concentration, from feeling. I hear cattle bawling somewhere in the north pasture, and coyotes again, and the wind in the screens all night.

Coal Pit

A long ride today, packing our lunch. We go east into the forest, then begin climbing upward. We tell our altitude by the change in vegetation. It is odd that now I am the one asked to identify plants. Four years ago I hardly knew one cactus from another. Now I can name the wildflowers under my feet, the vines, the parasites, the bushes and trees, ticking off names like a guidebook. But it hasn't been easy. So few people know the names of things, or know them wrong. I have had to do research, track down species, photograph them, preserve them, or retain them in my mind until I could find a photograph or a reliable source.

It was Archie who, one cold December day, gave me my first name, my first hint of this new world. I had been fascinated by the shining yellow globes that hung from a brittle plant growing everywhere. The yellow was vivid in the taupe fields, the only real color except for the ever-present red dust, the purple mountains.

I made my first trip down the road to

Archie's, and I looked at him with wonder — cowboy, survivor, son of Mormons, source of wisdom I needed. For a long while I was too shy to speak. I listened while he talked about his favorite subject: the changes that have taken place on this land of his. I looked and listened, my mind and body sponges, soaking up words, impressions, the sounds of the windmill, the wind blowing down the long valley and turning the silver blades.

Finally I gathered my courage, unfolded my hand that was filled with the yellow pods. "Please," I said, "can you tell me what this is?"

He looked at me kindly as if he were pleased with my curiosity. "Bull nettle," he said. "The Indians used the seeds to make cheese."

With his words, time opened, another distant world came into view, one I knew I had to learn. Plants, roots, reasons for things that were important. I needed to learn the West, its people. I did not know why these hungers suddenly took precedence. I still do not. I only knew that they did.

Bull nettle. Odd words to seal one's fate.

From that day I set out to learn a place and a way of life, and in so doing to learn more of myself and of poetry. I am not sure how any of this fits together, what I will do with my somewhat eclectic knowledge, but as Woodie calls back to me — "What's that flower?" — and I answer — "Scarlet bouvardia." — or as I explain the narcotic properties of the datura, most beautiful of poisonous plants, as I go out and gather the fruit of the agave, the roots of grass, something in me says: "Yes."

Suddenly, seeing the long needles of Apache pine, the red-stemmed manzanita, I realize we are on the way to Coal Pit, one of my favorite places.

The last miles we go single file over a path that is nothing but rubble, with the hill falling off several hundred feet at our left. The horses climb carefully, wanting a fall no more than we. I give Laddie his head, and he stretches his neck, sniffs the ground, puts his feet down with the caution of a true mountain horse.

Up, up, around a bend, and then we go down into a green meadow where cattle are grazing. Someone, perhaps Archie's brother-in-law, has leased the grazing rights in this part of the national forest. His stock pens are lower down; his cattle roam every-where.

Al told me that once there was a lumber camp here and that Archie helped to build the narrow road to the dam. Archie says, however, that the dam was simply a scheme to divert water from Cottonwood to Turkey Creek, and that the project was abandoned because of the squabbling of ranchers. Everything here begins and ends with water. People can and have murdered over it, something few in the East can understand.

Coal Pit always startles. It is a landscape from a fantasy, a painting nearly surreal. The high rhyolite cliffs suddenly separate, permitting the flow of water that forms a still pool at the dam's edge. In summer it is full, darkened by an accumulation of leaves. Unruffled, it is a perfect mirror of lichened cliffs. A tree with three forks stands bare in the center, branch rising into branch, trunk into trunk with no beginning and no end, only tree and image of tree, neither more real than the other.

Dragonflies, red and brilliant blue, make erratic tracks over the surface. Algae are thick, green, gluey at the edge. Striped snakes swim in sinuous ripples, making no sound. A young one has been drowned and floats at the edge, caught in the stems of grasses. Its smallness hurts me, its vulnerability in death.

I pull a dragonfly from the algae. It was caught fast in the glue, but working carefully I free first a shining wing, then four feet, then another wing. I admire the pattern, turquoise as brilliant as any Navajo stone, shiny black in alternating bands from head to the end of the long, down-curved tail. When I finish, it lights on my knee, preens, cleans its head with one foot then another. It thrums translucent wings in the wind that is constant down the cañon. It seems reluctant to fly, crawls up my jeans, shaking itself as any animal caught in rain or mud will do. I have always wanted to hold one, to capture, even momentarily, the dazzle, the blue streaking, the swift swirl of stained-glass wings.

When it flies, low over its reflection, I am bereft. To hold is not to have. To hold is to rejoice for one quick slice of time before one is alone again, lost to flight and the opening of patterns. The dragonfly returns, however, circles me as if in thanks for life, for a second chance to mimic sky and water, and I know a fierce and rational joy that will never leave me, that I will remember years from now buried in paper and books at my desk.

Returning down the mountain, I ride far behind, lost in thoughts. I talk out loud to Laddie who twitches his ears and seems to be agreeing.

The question of the Muse has been bothering me for some time. Historically the Muse has been female, the White Goddess, the exclusive property of men as, indeed, living by the pen was primarily a male occupation. But the increasing number of women writers demands a different perception of the Muse.

We must, I think, accept the fact that the Muse can be male, or perhaps be neither male nor female but sexless, as the human soul. Certainly a catalyst can be of either sex or not human at all, and Muses act as catalysts, impelling us inward and outward by the fact of their being. A tree, a rock, my dragonfly, all can be Muses, triggering a flash of insight, a moment of intuiting beyond what we are capable of seeing. The Muse is the property of dreams, and in this lies his/her power. Muses are heroes, goddesses in masquerade. They swoop down, like Jupiter, impregnate us, and vanish, and, although we may demand their return, weep for them, we retain the best part — inspiration, the creative force engendered by their passing.

Oddly, most of my Muses have been men, all have made me aware of different properties in myself, given me new perspective on the world.

There are, I know, women who would argue this with me, and I have no rebuttal save that the Muse is a personal thing, and that I, being as I am, need the force of an opposite to bring me to sight.

Old hermit that he is, Archie is Muse in a strange guise, but he receives it in the proper spirit. Muses always know what they are, always hear the unspoken dialogue.

"What do you think?" I ask Laddie, and he, in a familiar gesture, stops, curves his neck to nuzzle the toe of my boot. One day perhaps he, too, will serve a turn as Muse. For now, we are far behind the others, and the trail stretches ahead, smooth and sandy. I settle my hat and say: "Laddie, let's canter." And we do.

Back History

Like everyone else of my generation, I grew up with a romanticized version of the American West. A cowboy was Roy Rogers or Gene Autry, fresh-faced, clean, riding a wedding cake horse and singing while chasing rustlers. At the end of the chase he rode off, victorious, into the sage, hand in hand with a clean, fresh-faced woman chosen more because she looked like everywoman than for her acting ability.

Bad guys wore black and rode black horses. Good guys dressed in white and had the horses out of the picture books. Indians were naked or, at most, covered with a blanket. They shot up wagon trains, took scalps, spoke a preposterous pidgin English, and dragged all the pretty ladies riding the wagons through the dust. A cattle roundup lasted, on screen, at most ten minutes, and no one ever choked on the dust, sweated, bled, broke a foot, or had a hand smashed by a piece of machinery or a finger severed by dallying a rope. At the end of a hard day, everyone sat around a fire and sang songs about the glorious West.

Closer to the border, there were the Mexicans. Short, dark, greasy, they wore sombreros and said *"señor"* a lot. They lived in dusty little adobe towns, each with resident friar, central fountain, burros, and two kinds of women: those in black with shawls over their heads, and those in low-cut blouses that barely covered erupting bosoms. The latter had flashing eyes, teeth, and earrings, and were supposed to convey a wicked sensuality peculiar to Latins.

Back to the wagon train and its bevy of female paragons: gorgeous ladies who drove six-horse teams, golden curls a-tumble, pristine, starched, toothy. A streak of dirt across one rouged cheek indicated a hard day. No one, as I recall, ever indicated that they had to go to the bathroom and that the bathroom was behind the nearest mesquite or cactus, that they were having a period and would kill for a shot of laudanum or Lydia Pinkham compound which, then was mainly opium derivative, or that they were in labor, possibly dying. The nearest the movies came to such an event was the sound of an infant wailing from within the canvas walls of a Conestoga wagon accompanied by the appropriate music.

Cut to the ranch house, the homestead.

No sod hut with grass sprouting from the roof, no lean-to made of canvas and whatever else came to hand, but a sprawling place of huge logs with stone fireplaces, tables set with fine china and linen, and Chinese cooks grinning from miraculous kitchens. Outside, a fenced corral empty of manure and flies and filled with blooded horses rarely seen in the 19th-century West, a painted mountain, a lush field. Beauty. Perfection. Grace. The fairy tale in which we all share a part.

All of it wrong except for the land, the scenery that needs no script, that no make-up man or prop painter can distort. Something, however, has distorted it.

Archie says: "People come out here and say how beautiful it is. I see it as a desert. There's trees, flowers, animals that aren't here any more. That are just gone. Used to be we had rain twelve months a year, and grass high as a man's stirrups. I could look out and see it rippling just like a sea, and cattle moving through it. It grew so thick you never stepped on the ground but on the stems, and there were snakes, blue racers, that rode on the tops of the grass. You could see them coming from far away, coming so fast they never fell. And when I was young I'd see them and duck down and hide, but they'd find the hole and come right to it. Circle around the top a couple times, lookin' down at me. Then they'd go off, riding the swells till I couldn't see them any more. . . ."

It is mid-afternoon. The blinds creak in the wind, the sun comes in around them. We are talking idly, lazily, reminiscently about the past, more real to him now than the present.

We are talking about snakes, about how once a blue racer eight feet long fell out of a tree and wrapped itself around him. "And my hound dog went to barking and biting, and the snake kept squeezing and a bangin' its tail just like a whip till I was black and blue all over."

I, growing up in the country, had a similar experience, stepping on a black snake that coiled around my leg, foot to thigh.

He nods. "There's just somethin' about a snake. You can accept them, but once you touch one, it turns you."

He says when he was a boy they'd see rattlers twelve feet long and big around as a man's arm. That once his father showed him a female snake that rattled, calling her babies to her, then opened her jaws and swallowed them to keep them safe, later vomiting them out. He says he's seen this several times. I don't know if this is true. On the other hand, I don't know if it's false, either, and it makes a good tale.

His low voice goes on. Crickets and locusts shrill in the grass. Light falls in squares on the old, flowered carpet. The yellow cat peers in the door. It is a timeless day, the essence of all summer days.

"Tell me what it was like," I say. "Tell me."

He needs no urging. He goes on as if in a dream.

"We were self-sufficient. We raised everything we needed, even sugar cane. The climate was right then. Only thing we didn't have was salt, and we could trade for that. Pigs, cattle, chickens . . . we even learned how to can milk, and that was a help, not needing to keep it cool. Mexican woodcutters were here then, cutting wood for the mines. The men would come and work a while, and then bring up their wives. They were good people. My ma used to leave me with them when she went to town. Later on, when I went to school, I learned the real Spanish, the right way, verbs and tenses and then the words for things. Not like they teach now. . . ." His eyes are far away. He does not see me.

"This place was a sea of grass. In summer

56

the temperature hardly got above eighty-five. And in winter we had snow, real snow, started just after Thanksgiving. The tank would freeze solid. You could drive a team across, and skate, and sometimes the snow was thirty feet deep in the mountains." He sighs. "That's all gone now. Changed. The world's a different place. Nothing's like it was."

What happened to grass high as a man's stirrups? To grass so thick you never walked on the ground? To the plants and animals now gone forever?

"Partly overgrazing. Partly weather. The climate's changed. And now these jets. You can't tell me they don't change the weather. I've watched 'em. I know. I been watching the weather all my life, and I've stood right here and seen the rain clouds coming, and then one of those jets'll fly into it, break the sound barrier loud as thunder, and that rain cloud'll break up and drift away and form again up north, and that's where the rain'll fall. It's something big business and the government's doing. They got some reason. It's politics like everything else. They don't care for the land. They're all just lining their pockets."

No one has ever tried to talk Archie out of his airplane theory, partly, I suspect, because in voicing it he sounds so sure of himself, and partly because no one wants to intrude on an old man's rationalization of a world grown too large for him to comprehend.

His is the world of the past. Within our lifetimes this was the frontier. Here were homesteaders, cowboys, outlaws, one-room schoolhouses. Here, until after the Second World War, people lived as they had been living for a hundred years, without electricity, running water, or transportation other than horses and wagons. While all those movies that I so loved were being invented, while I was feeding on comic book myth, wild horses were running in Rucker Cañon, wolves were howling in the hills, rustlers were stealing cattle. Today they are still stealing cattle. Last week, down on the flats, a rancher lost two hundred head. The thieves came in trucks at night, loaded them, and drove away, probably slaughtering on the road and leaving no trace.

Archie says: "A man always carried a gun then. If you were out riding and saw someone coming toward you, you stopped and watched him. You pulled over. Gave him room. Looked at his face and hands and got the idea. Even if you knew him." He chuckles. "No one ever bothered me. Never had much money. Never had any at all until I was in my twenties. Didn't need it. A man traded for what he needed. Many times I slept out on these hills. Just rolled up in a blanket. Sometimes I'd wake up and there'd be three, four inches of snow on top of me. Kept me warm."

He looks at me. "You ever see my photographs?"

I have. One night last summer he came to supper bringing his tin biscuit boxes filled with them. He remembered every face, every horse, dog, and chicken, and told stories about them. My favorite is about the Indian and the outlaw, Clyde. "Show me the one of the three outlaws," I say. "The ones who killed Tar Wilson."

"Now that's a story." He gets up, goes into his bedroom, returns with a box. He shuffles through his memories for a minute and comes up with the photograph of the three men, handsome fellows and well-dressed.

Kick another myth. These outlaws wear silk shirts, good black boots, jaunty scarves. Their trousers are black broadcloth from the look of them. They are clean-shaven. Only their eyes give them away. All three have light eyes that look coldly into the distance, away from the camera. They are the eyes of killers, devoid of compassion.

"Tell me that story again," I beg.

He needs no urging. It is one of his favorites. He leans back, lights a Camel. "Well," he begins, his eyes following the dance of the smoke, "well, you remember how I told you my dad had a blacksmith shop. He fixed what needed fixing and didn't ask questions. Safer that way. Well, there was this old Apache, didn't have no name, or if he did, we didn't know it. Anyway, that Indian was just fascinated by blacksmithing. Every day he'd come down out of the mountains, driving a buckboard. And he was clean. Cleanest Indian I ever saw, always with a fancy buckskin shirt and this big high stovepipe hat. And he'd come in and just sit in the shop all day, watchin'. Not sayin' anything, just watchin'. Sometimes he'd take a piece of jerky if we offered it, and go to chewin'. And my dad, he had a bucket of some chemical he'd dip his hands in so he could lift hot iron and not get burned, and that Indian knew it." He tilts back further in his old chair, still watching the spiraling smoke. "So one day Clyde comes in with a broken bit needed fixin', and he sees that Indian, and he says . . . 'Hey. I bet you can't pick up that iron and walk with it like that. I bet five dollars.' And that old Indian stands up straight, and he picks up a piece of hot iron right off the forge and walks to the water with it just a-burnin' in his hand. And then he turns around and walks right up to Clyde, a-holdin' out his hand burnt black. And Clyde, well, he was a coward, see, and he takes one look at that Indian's face, and puts five dollars down and runs away."

He cocks his head and grins at me, building the suspense until I speak. "Then what?"

"Well, that Clyde was a dandy, always dressed fit to kill. He always wore a pair of leather gauntlets with silver decorations. And when he talked, he'd take them off and go to slappin' his palm with them. Slap, slap, like that. And one day he comes in and gets to boastin' how my dad's dry well was a good place to hide a body. And he's a slappin' his palm and talkin' big. Well, that night my dad went for the sheriff, and they rode out and pulled Tar Wilson's body out of that well, feet first. There was three of 'em in on it. Luther Price, Bill Tucker, and Clyde, and they killed Tar down at a little store used to be just off the road. Luther took the rap. Got hanged. Bill ran off to California and got hanged later. Raped a girl, I heard. And Clyde, well, Clyde disappeared. And I always thought it was that Indian got him. Tracked him back in the hills some- where and lifted his scalp. Those gloves, too, maybe. He was Apache. He never forgot."

We sit in silence. The mare and colt move past the window, tails swishing.

"What's the longest you been in the saddle?" he asks suddenly.

"I guess eight, ten hours," I say proudly.

"Humph," he says, eyes twinkling. Still, I see, I am a dude. "Used to be when I was riding for the Bates Ranch I'd go out before first light and ride all day. Not get back before the moon come up. I had a pack of hounds then, good cattle dogs, and five horses I kept fed up. I was doing a head count. The old man had bought that place, stock and all, and I found he'd got a hun- dred head more than he paid for. Took me thirty straight days."

I can't top that. Eighteen hours a day for thirty days doesn't leave time for much else, for singing songs at a fireside, for looking glamorous. The fact is there was no glamour. There was work. There was play only when the work was done. One survived here, or one died. And, alone with the wil- derness, one came to understand magnifi- cence.

As a writer a burden has been placed on

me. There is no point in perpetuating the myth, stringing fictions together to lead readers astray. There is no point to romance or even murder unless they serve to intensify what was real, to underscore the truth of what Archie calls "back history," the perilous journeys of men and women trying to live with dignity.

I think I will never again write in a spirit of frivolity, never again be satisfied with the graceful flowing of lies. I will have to learn that dark cavern of heart and body where truth lives. I will have to dig even to find the door to that cavern. It will be a difficult journey.

Today Archie brought out his seed treasures: red and white pinto beans in a crackled glass jar; heads of sunflowers bigger than my hand; another jar with "beans they don't have any more, just like they don't have tomatoes like they used to."

He shook them out into my hands, hard and shiny as jewels, and he gave me one of the sunflower seed-heads so I can try to raise my own. "Ten feet high at least," he promised, passing these life symbols with gnarled hands.

For years he has refused the idea of putting down his memories, has refused to talk to writers or historians, to share what he knows and remembers. I have never told him that I write, that I cherish what he tells me, yet somehow I think he realizes what I do.

Yesterday, trying to find something that will occupy him, keep his mind off his ill health, I told him he should write a book.

"No," he said. "I don't have the gift."

"Then tape it. You can talk."

He shook his head. "I won't. Because it wouldn't be the truth. It would only be my words, be what I remember. It wouldn't be enough."

What is truth? And how many truths can be told about the same event? This is the basis of fiction, the insurmountable wall of poetry, the road to Jung's collective unconscious. I could not argue with him without a good deal of thought, without confessing that, for years, I have been writing down his stories.

I could not say that the passing down of history ensures the continuation of life, gives security to the young, purpose to the old. That his stories and musings have become necessity for me, as if, in the hearing, I tap into the flowing of the world. Almost I know what shall be. I know pain is not my property alone, or joy, either. I know

64

the world goes on, shaped by those upon it, who are likewise formed by the land on which they live. I know that joy is there for the taking, for the reaching out. It is a gift. It is free. We have only to look. I have only to learn to see.

Roundup

Up at five. Darkness lifts early now, and this is the only state without Daylight Savings Time. The sky is fragile. Clouds linger at the top of mountains.

We meet Don in his field. He and his wife, Margaret, have camped out along the wash. Another rider has arrived, pulling a horse trailer, his horse already saddled within.

Margaret offers us ranch coffee, brewed over an open fire and tasting, in the clear mountain air, as delicious as a robust red wine. Don gives us our orders. I am to ride with him along the wash.

By now Laddie knows the game and plays like a pro. He finds cattle by instinct, moves them out of brush and hollow with a bossy glee that is exciting to watch and to ride. I am, I realize suddenly, as at home in the saddle as one born to it. My body whips back and forth as if I am an extension of the horse. I do not seem to need reins but guide him with knees and weight. We drive a few head downpasture, whipping from side to side to keep them bunched, and meet Don who has rounded up more.

We start them toward the corral, a surge of mottled, plunging bodies, a sea of backs, tails, tossings. At the far end of the field they break, peel off, scatter fast as birds. The old Brahma bull, spotted black and white like a hound and with a hump on his back, is declaring his possession of these females, of these leaping babies. He stands immobile, and his huge presence, his aura of kingship, turns them right, left, back the way they came in a blind panic.

"That son-of-a-bitch is turning them!" Don yells. Cinco moves from a walk to full gallop, her sooty legs flashing above grass and dust. Laddie and I do the same, heading them off at the other side, darting, galloping, changing direction in mid-stride, mid-air. It is like flying. I do not even feel the beat of his run, only the long smooth rush of motion.

Again we move, again try to stem the turn, the flight away from the Minotaur. He is a force, a silent power, his very stillness a challenge, a taunt. He watches us, and his eyes say we are fools.

"Get that dang bull out of there!" Don shouts, on his way after a group of frightened mothers headed for the shelter of the wash. We bear down on him. He stares, disdainful. Laddie darts, feints, finally reaches out, quick as a snake, and nips the spotted rump. The creature bellows, moves out slowly. He will not run. He is too old, too conscious of himself as king. He ambles as if we are not there or are no more than flies buzzing at his rear. He switches his tail, bellows again, and defecates. Laddie quivers but keeps on pushing until we have him down the field and into the corral.

"You look like a real cowboy!" Margaret calls as we lope back to the herd. And something is born in me right there in the field with the grass bending down, the cattle coming up it — black, brown, spotted, frantic. With the wind dividing, going past on either side of me. With the sun, focused now, giant, heated eye, firing all beneath it.

Past, present, future congeal. I am alive, born, woman, centaur, flowing of time, part of a great and constant streaming. It is one of those moments of absolute unity, of complete faith. I am doing what I was meant to do. Somehow, here on this horse, in this morning with its heat, dust, noise, with the rhythm of ongoing motion, with this body that blends into, springs out of self and creature, that will neither fall nor be trampled, I am doing what was meant from the beginning, what I, unknowing, searched for and found.

The overworked, subservient housewife is gone. In her place, I am, woman of words, woman of capabilities suddenly discovered. "Yes," I say, accepting. "Yes." And Laddie, attuned to every nuance, moves faster, ecstatic arrow, toward the bawling and muscular sea.

The others come down off the mountain. They have lost two cows and a calf somewhere in the maze of rock, cañons, mesquite thickets. We all go, spreading out and up the side of a hill, and down past springs, around clumps of Spanish bayonet and cholla. Jays flutter and squawk. Hawks rip the silence. We search hollows, miniature cañons, hillsides mined with rocks that roll beneath hoofs. This is hard riding, and it is hot. I think of water, rain, snow. A sweat breaks out on Laddie's neck, darkening his red hide. He moves with deliberation. The dazzle, the arc into myth has gone.

At last someone yells: "There they are!" I see a flash of mahogany hide against umber rocks as the three fugitives run ahead of us. We give chase, spattering sunflowers and tar weed like jewels.

It comes again, the feeling of abandon. The horse is running for the joy of it, reaching, catching, reaching, catching, through yellow flowers, through gray-stemmed tallow, through grama, blue air, his neck extended, his ears laid flat, his tail streaming behind.

And on through the afternoon, the sun a frying pan on fire in the sky. Cattle crowd in the pens and the chute, bawling, mooing, shrieking. Huge, dumb mamas refuse to move, to go forward or back even when whacked with a two-by-four or shot with a cattle prod. Hysterical, they stand bawling, trampling the babies that run behind them, frustrating the humans outside the rails.

Kick, trample, cry out, fight back. The noise, the stink wrap around us. We sweat, bleed, turn black and blue, nurse wasp stings, rope burns. We curse, cut, jab, smear, burn letters into living flesh, staple tags into hairy ears. I work the head chute, a complicated affair of levers and gears that catches the animals by the neck and renders them helpless. I work it with my whole weight, my whole body, until I am reeling. My head aches with the noise, the glare of the sun, the demands on unused muscles and the necessity to co-ordinate hands, feet, and mind in a series of related but unfamiliar motions.

The mamas, inoculated and ear-tagged,

stand in a circle and call for their calves. Like robots set into action, they don't stop. Their mouths open and close, open and close without thought.

The little ones, sexless now, burned and bloodied, stagger from the chute and seek their mothers. They nurse and flee to the hills. They hurt. They cry. They run, leaving trails of blood on the sand.

By nightfall there is silence. And the stench of burned hide, of cow dung. There are mounds of it everywhere, green and drying to dust.

No one speaks on the way home. The horses drag their heads. We have lived another life for twelve hours. We have seen the reality of cattle raising and are possessed by it, our bodies stiff and numb.

As we top the rise near the corrals, the darkness comes down quick and final, like a knife.

Edith

Archie's sister Edith is a square woman with startling blue eyes in a tanned face and a radiant smile. She knows the names and uses of every plant in these mountains, and she has kept careful records of births, deaths, all of the lives in the county around her.

I first met her at a ranch barbecue. We started talking about herbs and flowers, about the pot of curving, scented lilies she had brought as a gift, and were soon lost in the warmth of a new friendship. We were at one of the tables talking around mouthfuls of succulent ranch beans and grilled steak when suddenly she looked up from her plate. "The heck with this eating," she said. She chuckled. "Won't hurt me to miss a meal. Let's take a nature walk."

I wish I had a photograph of us on that evening. The old woman teaching knowledge to the younger, bending down to pull and pick with the mountains growing dark all around, the sky in the west a vivid, almost liquid yellow. This is how all learning takes place, through the listening, the seeing, the performing of acts. This is how shamans learned their arts, and I come to it naturally, eagerly, hands outstretched.

She showed me what she called "nut grass," a slender blade attached to a brown bulb. After rubbing it free of earth, she offered it to me. "Eat it," she said. "It's good. Like a nut."

I took it, not without misgiving, for, after all, I did not know her, or the extent of her knowledge, and in the fading light she seemed to grow larger, more powerful than a mere ranch wife. I took it, though, crunching the root in my teeth. It tasted from earth and sun. It was like chewing the seasons. I made a wish on it — that I would return here again and again.

Watching me, she chuckled again. "Turkeys used to love that plant. Back when I was growing up, there were so many turkeys. Sometimes we'd ride up here looking for cattle, and the whole hill would go to gobbling."

Hence, I suppose, the name Turkey Creek. I remember that the Apaches would not eat turkeys, supposing that they fed upon snakes. And so they multiplied, ran wild, set the mountains to gobbling. Strange that now there are so few. They have been hunted, reduced in numbers like so many other species. The wolves are gone, and the jaguars. And, although every now and then you hear about the sighting of a mountain lion, no one I knew has ever seen one in the wild.

Over the years, Edith and I write letters. She tells me of climate and what is growing, and I tell her the same from where I am, and the link between us, our fascination, our love of growing things deepens as does our friendship. She has the eternal qualities of an Earth Mother, even though Archie once said of her: "Edith! She's so ornery she ought to be put out of her misery." I have never told her this. I do not intrude in a long-established sibling rivalry that seems to be mostly one-sided. Edith is always sending Archie milk puddings and casseroles that he refuses to eat, and for which she gets no thanks. "Women think they can cure anything with enough food," he says. "Well, they can't." I have never told her this, either.

Today I will visit her. I drive off the mountains onto the first flatlands of the valley. The bare flanks of the Swisshelm Mountains rise in front of me as I turn off onto a small road winding in and out of mesquite, cholla, and clumps of tall grama. I can't see the house until I am almost upon it, as is often the case with the houses of good witches who live in the woods.

It is a square house, a typical territorial one of stuccoed adobe. It has a metal roof, a narrow porch running on all four sides, and plants growing everywhere. Oxalis is in bloom in the shade. A trumpet vine twines thickly around the front columns, its flowers red-orange with long and succulent throats. The green leaves of poinsettias growing in pots make a hedge against the railing. The yard is a jungle of grass, lilac bushes taller than my head, and elm trees with giant roots stretching in all directions.

Edith comes out radiating welcome. We hug as if only through touch can we proclaim our friendship. She takes my arm and shows me her fenced garden, her almond tree that she started from a seed. It is thirty feet tall now, and sturdy. "No need for more than one," she says. "They cross-fertilize with the peaches." And I store that knowledge away to be used, treasured.

She leads me to the house. The walls are thick. The vines shade the windows; the old fashioned kitchen is green and cool. Peaches are stacked everywhere. It is, obviously, harvest time.

The house holds the accumulated interests of her varied life. There is not a clear space anywhere. Tables overflow with pictures, books, colored stones, seashells, plates of candy and nuts, needles and thread, old letters, new magazines. Firewood is stacked in an unused bedroom where jars of peaches and okra line the shelves. More peaches are in boxes on the floor. The room is a sea of golden balls.

"I got more peaches this year," she says. "You take some back for you and Jeanne."

Her friend Nadine sits on the edge of a chair, a basket in her lap. They are going pear picking. I look at Nadine, trying to find in her plain, brown-eyed face some hint of the woman who stole a man away from his wife and lived with him and his seventeen cats in the state of adultery until his death. I am foiled. She looks like no adulteress I ever saw or imagined. Her elbows are as bony as her knees, and several front teeth are missing. She doesn't say much, simply listens to Edith and me, smiling once in a while with lowered eyes.

"That's the best old pear tree," Edith says. "And it just grew. Here, I saved you one from last time." She hands me a dish with a golden pear and a knife. I don't have the heart to say I don't like pears, so I cut it into four pieces and take a bite. This is not pear. It is pure sun. I am mesmerized. Juice runs from the corners of my mouth and down my chin, and I follow it with my tongue. I am lost in pear. I shall never eat another. The lingering essence of this curved fruit will last a lifetime.

Edith is an observer, a diary-keeper. Instinctively she knows the value of the past, and she has kept sparse but careful records of births, deaths, marriages, and events. Names and dates are all noted in her neat hand. Photographs of schoolmates, of the old school house, of children, grandchildren, brothers and sisters are all carefully labeled in her large albums.

She piles them on my lap, and from that moment nothing else seems important. I read her entries, see life as it was: Edith driving the wagon into the hills to cut wood; gathering eggs from the flock of white leghorns; dressing for dances at a town called Lights, a town which has disappeared into the desert; Edith rounding up cattle, chasing rattlesnakes from the kitchen with the handle of a broom, walking to the one-room school over the fields I now ride, the grasshoppers so thick her bare feet were covered with their juice.

One entry states: **Bought eighteen dozen clothespins at the store.** I try to do the mental arithmetic. How many clothespins is that? Who would need so many? What vast amount of wash was done by hand in a tin tub over a fire? I try to visualize it: the heating of water, the scrubbing, the hanging out. The ironing done with heated flatirons. The diapers, work clothes, Sunday best shirts, blouses, ruffled petticoats.

I think of the rôles of women. No stereotypes in this rough country. No clinging vines and fewer whiners. Women worked as hard as men. They rode, shot, rounded up cattle. They cooked, cleaned, cut wood, bore children, lots of them and often alone. They danced, mourned the dead, and cared for the dying with what remedies they knew.

I think about the women who made the overland journey by wagon; about those who walked pushing handcarts across the prairie; about those who taught school, did laundry, worked as prostitutes to stay alive; about the woman in Texas who painted a piano keyboard on paper and taught her children to play. About women who lived, fought, loved, and died, the equals of their men.

What we in this century know of the last has become fantasy. We have mythologized outlaws and heroes to the point of distorting our own history. And we have made light of the women who labored beside them.

I am still deep in thought when Edith takes me outside to show me the skunks that have nested on her porch, that play like kittens around her feet each evening when she sits there and watches the sun go down. She shows me her turtles, too, great, hard-shelled creatures that, one by one and in pairs, appear each afternoon for their dinner of dry cat food.

She talks. Her words spill out and over me. There is so much to learn, so much I have to do.

Death

I am standing in the yellow kitchen of a rented apartment in Minneapolis, listening to my son read the mail to me over the telephone.

"Here's a letter from Jeanne," he says.

And I say: "Oh, good. What's she say?"

" 'I hate having to write this,' " he reads in his slow fashion, " 'but we found Archie dead early this morning. He died peacefully in his sleep on the couch with his Bible beside him. He wanted to be cremated, his ashes scattered here. I know you will miss him as much as we will.' "

Archie dead? How can that be? In two weeks I would have been there. "Why couldn't he have waited?" I say foolishly to no one in particular. "Why couldn't he?"

In snatches I remember tales, words, actions. They play over the yellow walls like a silent film. I remember washing Archie's dishes, hefting a ten-gallon enamel tea kettle with both hands, pouring hot rinse water, and wondering if his women were stronger, with huge hands, muscled arms, shoulders of iron.

I remember his tale of the albino wolf that ran alone on silent paws. Of how, when finally trapped, it refused to die and sprang at its pursuer, dragging the trap behind.

And the story of the Lee boys who, with a pack of lion dogs, hunted jaguar until there were few of the spotted cats on this side of the border.

I remember Archie's treasures — the silver-mounted bridle, relic of Villa's war, that he found in the desert near Agua Prieta on the skeleton of a horse; his boxes of photographs; the rose bush that had been his mother's; the mare, the foal, the yellow cat, Pete the mule.

I remember the recipes for pickled pork, for beans with ham hocks, for stews and snakebite; the lessons in how to hold the reins, how to bridle; the day I bridled the mare and she whirled and took off kicking, a shrewish female unused to others of her sex. I remember the old ways going faster now, streaming down the valley like the wind, and me, running after, crying: "Wait! Wait for me!"

But nothing waits, not time, or dying, or happiness. Happiness we must take when it comes, savor it, treasure it, for gifts come rarely, friendship more rarely still.

I remember myself serving lunch in a

hurry before we went off to doctor a sick horse. "Don't wait," I said, slapping plates down on the table, and he, with a grin, answering: "I'm waitin' on you like one hog waits on another."

So he did not wait. What use is it when you are crammed into a body you consider useless, forced to accept charity from neighbors, family you have not spoken to in years? You do not wait. You say — "Go it." — and you take your leave, knowing your ashes will be here, in the red dust, beside the changing mountains, under the blue enamel sky. Your bones will be here and the sound of your voice saying: "Used to be. . . ."

Nothing will bring him back. He has gone behind a barrier I can neither see nor cross. To mourn ostentatiously is out of the question. I would be mourning for myself. I recall tears shed by others at gravesides, in funeral parlors, and realize that such grief is not for the dead but for the living.

So I will not cry. I will write, having learned one last and poignant lesson from my friend, my Muse.

Part Two

Metamorphosis
1986–1988

Metamorphosis

I am headed south out of Tombstone, driving fast. It's a town I don't like, a town that is now more like Coney Island than the brawling boomtown of miners, whores, outlaws and Earps that it was. But it is still violent. Many say it is cursed.

I'm glad to be leaving. I have spent the past few days delving into history, **Walking Where They Fell**, as the signs proclaim. (Falsely, as it turns out. The famous OK Corral gunfight took place in what is now part of Highway 80.) The thought of dinner and good conversation with an old friend from ranch days is more appealing at this moment than arid research.

The road winds down into Government Draw. The San Pedro Valley sprawls to my right, the purple Mule Mountains beckon ahead. It is near sunset on a gentle February day.

The valley stretches into infinity, and the sky, flushed rose and apricot, lifts, hovers, surrounds the whole with delicate light. I am part of the inside of a shell, coming up and out of spiraled depths onto a great and shining plain, and my happiness, my unity with earth and sky, with a rift in the clouds that lets through a flood of gold is so intense that I stop the car and sit listening to the inner voice that speaks to me often.

"Stay west," it says, and there is urgency in the tone. "Don't go back. Stay here. Your life is here."

It reiterates what I already know. I have grown in this country, come to an understanding of self, and thus am part of it, caught willingly in its web.

Later, when I describe the moment to a friend who places her faith in earth's messages, she says: "You were touched by God. He showed you your place and your future. Please listen. Promise me."

My return East from this trip, paid for with money from a research grant, was by contrast joyless. I received no welcome, not even a polite show of interest about what I had seen or discovered. I remember most poignantly that the telephone was ringing as I paid off the taxi and entered the house. It was my husband telling me to be sure to mop the floor in the front hall, and that he would be late for dinner.

Why I hoped for anything else when this was the established pattern of a twenty-year marriage, I don't know, but I did. That evening, and most succeeding ones, I felt an increasing aloneness, the sorrow and sense of exhaustion that comes with failure. To survive at home I had, over the years, split myself in half, being two people, subservient wife and respected writer and teacher. Later I began to wonder about my own talent and ability, those things that were mine, alone, which satisfied me most. My husband at his best called my writing "a hobby." At his worst, when it interfered with what he presumed were his rights, he reminded me that he paid the taxes on what I earned and that he was, without any doubt, the head of the house.

Still I held on. An uncomprehending victim of psychological and verbal abuse, I somehow had managed to preserve the core of self where I existed, wrapped in a labyrinth of protective gestures and submissive behavior. No one had ever guessed my unhappiness or questioned my life.

Questioning was left for me, beginning with my earliest memories of childhood and following the slender thread of answers to the end. Was I worth saving? Was my existence valuable?

In retrospect this sounds ridiculous. Surely I knew my own worth? The fact is, that I did not. Like many women I had been raised to accept commands; I had been cast in a mold that had never fit and, made guilty because of my differences, had remained there, trapped by female tradition. The obedient child had become the obedient slave/wife almost to the point of annihilation.

Alone in my kitchen, I forced myself through formidable analysis. I argued, wept, questioned every command, action, and mood of self and of those close to me. Discovery followed discovery. The pattern was clear. All that was unique in my personality had been from the start viewed as threatening — by men and women, parents, teachers, even my husband. I had been shaped, forced into meekness by society's fear of the individual; I was a composite of the weakness of others.

Slowly the cocoon in which I had hidden began to open. Light filtered in, and hope. *Yes,* I had the right to life, to laughter, to the use of my own voice. These are inalienable rights — of the spirit — yet they are never handed to us. They must be worked for. They must be earned. What we begin with at birth is simply the right to try.

Behind these insights hovered a sense of history, the Western landscape in all its vastness, its terrible yet magnificent nakedness, its fragility. Painted on it, moving across its billowing surface, were images of the men and women who, driven by necessity as well as love of adventure, had conquered physical and mental hardship and survived.

The West had become part of me; we had exchanged bones, perhaps on that evening in Government Draw, perhaps earlier, during roundup, in the course of those lazy afternoons with Archie, or on walks across fecund fields with Edith. The West stimulated my consciousness, drew me out of a timid self into a larger one. It was, and is, a place where individuality is necessity not crime. As it had for so many others, it became for me the land of opportunity.

Even after I had made my decision, when I came to say good bye to my friends of a lifetime, those who towards the end had encouraged me, championed me, I was unprepared for their reaction. "You're the gutsiest woman I know," several said. I answered: "It's a question of living or dying. Guts have nothing to do with it."

Faced with death, of the body or the spirit, we must struggle, must fight the oppressor, for life and the soul are our most precious possessions.

Thus, early one morning, I walked out of the house which one visitor, in awe, had labeled "a museum," locked the door, and pointed my car toward the west. It was, oddly enough, the anniversary of D-Day — the sixth of June.

I had a job to do on my way, another grant in my pocket to enable me to find a trace of Mattie Earp, the second wife of Wyatt Earp, famous lawman, deserted by him for Josephine Sarah Marcus, a San Francisco beauty.

I followed Mattie's cold trail through the cow towns, the prairie towns, across Missouri and the surging plains of Kansas — a blind search for a woman who, despite all efforts, has remained a mystery.

On the way I kept a journal as so many prairie travelers had done before me.

Odyssey

Lamar, Missouri rises out of lush and rolling prairie. Purple coneflowers bloom by the roadsides, and the air is scented with sweet clover and honeysuckle. Newborn mules are leaping in pastures, and I stop, hang fascinated on a fence at the sight of the long-legged babies and the sleek mares that bore them.

I am beginning as close to the beginning of what is known about Mattie as I can. I know where she lived as a child, and where and how she died, and precious little else save that she was in Fort Scott, Kansas in 1870 and had her photograph taken. At the same time, Wyatt Earp, his mother, father, brothers, and sisters were in nearby Lamar, having arrived there in the spring of 1869.

Were it not for the old photograph and others found in Mattie's trunk at the time of her death, we wouldn't know of her existence except as a name on isolated documents. Were it not for the incredible luck and tireless research of Glenn Boyer, the secret of her trunk would have remained where it was — in the house of Mattie's nephew.

We would not know that she was a red head with a fiery temper, that she was the daughter of Elizabeth and Henry Blaylock, whose own photograph shows them in true American Gothic style: the wife long, lean, hair pulled back, uncompromising, humorless; the husband smaller, bearded, with a wicked grin hidden behind his beard.

Did Mattie run away from this grim mother, arrive in Fort Scott penniless, and turn to prostitution as a means of support? Like so many others, her wanderings have faded into the dust. Court records, the censuses, make no mention of her, either under her given name, Celia Ann Blaylock, or under the name by which she was known to the Earps — Mattie. I do not know how or where she met Wyatt, or if, indeed, they were ever legally married.

Less than half an hour after my arrival in Lamar, I am sitting at the round oak table in Reba Earp Young's cheerful kitchen. Reba is Wyatt's third cousin, a devoted keeper of family records, a tireless historian and a writer herself. We are going through family albums and genealogies, a priceless collection of photographs animated by Reba's recollections.

"We don't know much about Mattie," she says, "and just a little more about Urilla

Sutherland," referring to Wyatt's first wife whom he married in Lamar and who died shortly thereafter.

Over coffee we exchange theories and suppositions. "Look at that Josie," she says, referring to the scandalous photograph of the third and last Mrs. Wyatt Earp clothed in a veil and little else. "No wonder Wyatt left Mattie. But he got what he deserved. Josie was a conniving sneaky little devil."

"And Mattie? How did he meet her? What was she doing in Fort Scott?"

Reba shakes her head, looks at me with what can only be called, "Earp eyes," sharp, intelligent, missing little. "It's a sad story, but we don't know very much. She was over in Fort Scott. We know that. He could have met her there, it was the big market town for Lamar, and he was a teamster. But she was never in Lamar as far as I've been able to find out. And she could have been perfectly respectable in Fort Scott. Maybe she was living with relatives." She leafs through the album thinking. "But if she wasn't . . . well, there weren't many ways for girls to make a living back then, you know."

Times have changed for the better. In the 19th Century a female runaway had little chance. The pages of literature are filled with some of the more famous — Big Nose

Kate, Lottie Deno, Squirrel Tooth Alice — women who took the only way available to them. Not for the first time am I glad to have been born in the 20th Century.

I leave Reba with regret, go on to the courthouses of Nevada, Missouri and Fort Scott, Kansas, square, thick-walled buildings designed as lasting symbols of the proud advance of civilization. They guard the records of marriages, births, deaths, occupations, mortgages, records of millions of lives, and I pull the unwieldy old books from the shelves with a sense of excitement. Here, in fine copperplate handwriting, is a window on the past. I skim through lists of names — Adonija, Absalom Neptune, Americus, Jesephus, Anna Aurilla, Mahala, Julia Minorva, Thelezaim — names that would make a book all by themselves; names that indicate a wealth of classical and Biblical knowledge in those who bestowed them. But there is no Blaylock anywhere.

Outside it is sickly hot, the beginning of summer in Kansas. Thunderstorms break on the horizon. The land rises and falls, shimmering in the heat.

This is the weather our ancestors lived through without air conditioning, in sod houses and canvas tents, without the comforts of baths, the coolness of water save that drawn from creek or well. This is the land they crossed, they plowed behind mules and oxen without even a vision of today's reapers and threshers complete with stereo systems and cool air. This is the hard land upon which they survived or died, depending on their wits, the labor of their hands and backs, and sometimes on just plain luck.

On the steps of the courthouse I look at Mattie's Fort Scott photograph. "Damn you, Mattie!" I say. I stare at her and see a meanness in the square face, a petulance in the mouth, the whole expression that of a stubborn and not-too-bright child. And suddenly I think I know something. Suddenly I see this spoiled child filled with anger, hate, the refusal to please, to adapt, to make do. I see her, years later, standing on the porch of the little house on Freemont Street in Tombstone, knowing that Wyatt has fallen in love with Josie. Josie, who had a gaiety to match Wyatt's own and the same love of adventure. Josie, loving the man and not the opportunities. And I can see Mattie, her chin set, her eyes narrow, her skirts swishing the dust saying: "Go and be damned to you both."

And then time swallows her as if she were mirage, part of the dust, the glitter of

Tombstone, the little town on Goose Flats. Only the anger remains, and the hatred; enough so that, to forget Wyatt, or perhaps to spite him, she kills herself in Pinal six years later, drugged, drunken, despoiled by men.

These are fragments I intuit, picked up in the sand of the streets, in the unpaved alleys where tumbleweed piles against fences, in the faded splendor of Tombstone's Crystal Palace Saloon, in the jumble of junk in the Birdcage Variety Theater where once women danced and sang and swung from beribboned ropes dressed only in pink tights and spangles. Where, in the street near Fly's studio one October afternoon, Wyatt and his brothers shot it out with Clantons and McLaurys because that was what they had to do.

We all do what we must, heroes and villains, men and women alike. And sometimes in the doing echoes survive, heard by those who listen hard enough.

As I leave Kansas behind, as I catch my first sight of the Rocky Mountains on the western horizon and know I am, now, nearing home, I wonder what echoes I will leave behind.

Mirage

It rises from the flood plain of the Arkansas, out of place, out of time, a medieval castle keep, high-walled, with watch towers at the corners. Its immensity, its audacity in the midst of cactus-strewn prairie stands testimony to those who conceived, built, lived, worked in it. Few cowards or loafers among them, or fools, either.

Here the Bent brothers, William, George, and Charles, built a trading post and named it Bent's Fort. Here Kit Carson worked as hunter, trapper, man at home on the frontier in any guise. Here Susan Shelby Magoffin on her honeymoon trip across the plains stopped, rested, and wrote in her diary that the fort was her idea of "an ancient castle."

Names become reality laid in blocks of adobe that surround a city complete with stock pens, chicken coops, store rooms, living quarters and kitchens, and even a billiard room. Here, beyond the walls, the Cheyennes, the Arapahoes, the Comanches camped, danced, made up war parties, and traded the pelts of animals for white mans' goods brought over the Santa Fé Trail.

My route has been running parallel to the Santa Fé Trail, that old highway that was traveled by armies, by immigrant wagons, by traders and cattlemen, tinkers, trappers, outlaws, Indians, men of God, women and children, by everyone with the need or desire to reach the Southwest, so many travelers for so long that traces of the road remain, a mile wide and ground down to bedrock, a ribbon of history across the heartland of America.

From this immense fort, armies went forth to capture an empire from Mexico. Through here traders moved outward to Kansas City and St. Louis, to Taos, Santa Fé, Mexico City, California — more and more every year from the 1820s until after the Mexican War when the War Department offered William Bent $12,000 for the post. He refused with disdain, calling the offer ridiculous. He had, after all, given most of his life to the building and maintenance of the place.

In the fall of 1852, he loaded his family — his Cheyenne wife and four children — into wagons and moved them downriver. When they had gone, he blew his achievement to smithereens.

Fortunately enough drawings and plans of the fort remained, and it has been rebuilt, a red adobe mirage where, listening closely, I can hear woodchoppers' axes, the lowing of cattle and the jingle of harness, the wagons, wheels, hoof beats, diverse tongues of destiny.

I have almost forgotten why I am taking this immense journey. Perhaps it does not matter. All the books I devoured as a child come flooding back, the names of the famous, of places that heretofore existed only on the printed page.

Raton Pass, that high, treacherous entrance into New Mexico from the north, becomes reality as I push up the steep grade and watch the light on the dashboard flicker when the car overheats.

Wagons were unloaded here, double-teamed, hauled perilously to the top. Some tumbled thousands of feet into the gorges, taking the animals with them. Women and children disembarked and climbed the rocky road in all weathers. Now, despite the warning light, ways and means are simplified.

I reach the summit and pull over. New Mexico, the Land of Enchantment, lies below and as far south as I can see. And on this June day, beneath a sky so blue it burns the eyes, is a valley like a bowl reflecting sky. Everywhere, in all directions, flinging up in a frenzy from the ground, wild iris are blooming, a tapestry rolled out at my feet as if in welcome.

Acoma Pueblo

Route 40 leaves Albuquerque in a swirl of concrete, between stark shapes of metal warehouses. The temptation here is to speed, to put the evidence of humanity's tastelessness behind and reach the rolling plains that glide effortlessly into mesa country.

At the top of a long rise the earth opens into a succession of parallel mesas that run north-south and stretch westward, changing color as I look. Blue, lavender, red, ocher, they are living things, running horses, the wings of being that suddenly leap and follow.

At the top of this hill I come to believe in the possibility of flight. If I stretch out my arms, I will be free of earth and will ascend and look down from the height of sky. I will dream it, this place. It will be in me, talisman, the voice of mesas, the true song of my heart.

The road descends, a long, easy sloping, then rises again, and still space is before me, the space of the mind, of unlimited possibility. With hunger tempered by humility, I reach out to crevice, rock, elasticity of rock skeletons, vulnerable but lasting. Except for the road and a few Indian dwellings, no one has come to spoil this magnificence. Perhaps no one can. It is a state of mind rather than place, a reminder of the necessity for meeting challenges, and in that message, daunting.

At each crest, each change of color, my excitement rises. Closer to the mesas, my eye curves around their sides, memorizes them — texture, red-painted skin, power of thrust. At last I turn off for Acoma, Sky City, the mesa that has been inhabited for at least a thousand years by those Indians for whom air is home.

The day is windy. Grasses bend, chamiso flowers dip and toss until the plain is in motion, a yellow sea. The two mesas rear up from the ground like islands. The first, called "Enchanted," is deserted, the scene of a long-ago tragedy. A flash flood tore away the trail the Indians used to reach the top where they grew their gardens of squash, corn, and beans, and, unable to descend the steep sides, they perished there without shelter, food, or water, under the merciless sky.

The road that climbs the second mesa to Acoma is torturous, barely wide enough for two cars, and nearly vertical. There is no guardrail, no barrier, only rocks, holes, sand, and perilous turnings above a drop of hundreds of feet. I take the road because I must. There is no other entry.

Once at the top, I am free of fear. The sky is over and around me. The wind moves freely, unhampered by trees, buildings, shapes of earth. It is ever-present, and on this day is hard and fierce, thrumming in my ears, driving sparrows to shelter in holes in adobe walls.

Tourists are not allowed to wander freely here. They must register and wait for a guide. I stand with a gaggle of females, Eastern schoolteachers from their conversation that consists of ways and means of education for Indians, tidbits of history, comparisons of mementos bought on their trip. And then they look at me.

"Are you our guide?" one asks. I laugh with the young Indian girl who has stepped out of the office in time to hear the artless question.

"No," I tell her. "She is."

I am always being taken for Indian. I am used to it but tired of denial. The Sioux take me for Cheyenne, the Cheyenne think me Crow, the Crow believe me to be from these very pueblos of New Mexico.

The guide's name is Fern. She, too, believes me to be Indian, but she does not ask, only directs her statements to me as if we form a society of our own. Argument is useless. I nod and smile and gaze off over the edge into the rise and fall of distance.

"Today," she says, "we go back to the old ways. We learn the language from our grandfathers who are our dictionaries."

The schoolteachers murmur among themselves. Sacrilege? Un-American? Ungrateful? It is hard to know what they are thinking. Once more Fern and I exchange smiles. What can they know, these somehow foreign women who come to exclaim, poke at, whisper with manners as bad as the worst of students?

Here is the mission school, locked and empty. Here the church with its inside walls painted with symbols, ears of corn, flashes of lightning. And here the infamous bell tower.

"The bell in the tower was brought from Mexico. We paid for it. Two boys and two girls."

"Oh!" the women exclaim, without questioning who demanded such a payment. "Oh!"

Here the cliff over which, in the early 17th Century, *Padre* Baltazar was hurled by the ancestors of the present-day dwellers. For fifteen years the *padre* exercised his tyranny, grew fat from the produce of his gardens, the soil for which was carried up from the plain, the water in *ollas* from cisterns. When in anger *Padre* Baltazar struck and killed his serving boy, his tyranny came to an end. He was tossed over the edge of the mesa onto the rubble heap hundreds of feet below.

Fern does not mention this. Instead she points toward the north. A hundred miles distant, Mount Taylor, the sacred mountain from which the beams for the church roof were cut, looms dark in the clear air. She points again at the desiccated plain over which the men of the pueblo were forced to carry the beams.

The narrow streets wind, double back upon themselves. In sheltered doorways tables stand laden with pottery. The teachers browse among owls, seed-jars, double-necked wedding vases. Their voices are as shrill as those of the sparrows.

"Many of these pots come from Japan now," Fern says. "They come and we paint on them."

What happened to the potter's art? To the women shaping clay carefully, by hand, leaving their imprint, their mark? I turn away and buy fry bread and honey from a young woman who takes me into her kitchen. When I come out, one of the women approaches me. "Is it safe to eat?" she wants to know.

I can't answer. I only know that it is good, that it warms me, and that the honey tastes like sweetened gold. I shrug and gesture, and she returns to ponder possible purchases.

No one reprimands me when I wander off alone. I stand at the edge a long time, eye to eye with eagles.

Santo Domingo Pueblo

Tumbleweeds bounce across the road, skittish as horses. Mica sparkles in the sand, and the summer air dazzles. Impatient for secrets, I drive toward the Río Grande that tumbles like a stream of diamonds flowing south. A few children and dogs play at its edge. They shriek and watch me — white woman in a city car. I feel my own strangeness. I do not belong, and yet in my own way I do.

The village is haphazard. Houses sprout, disintegrate, and are abandoned. The effect is one of careless abstraction, jumbled squares and rectangles erected, then falling down.

I leave the car under an elm beside the church plaza. The ground here is worn smooth from centuries of processions and dancing, and is lower than that where I stand. Overhead in the leaves, birds fuss and twitter over my presence.

A gate leads to the churchyard. I stand before it staring at the small adobe mission, at the painting above its door. No abstraction here. Two spotted horses, one black, the other brown, face each other, nose to nose. Behind them a painted sky, a blue that defies belief.

"Impossible," I say to myself. But it is not. I have seen this sky many times. It is the sky of the Southwest, an impenetrable, magical blue.

An old man wrapped in a rainbow of blankets and wearing a battered felt hat stops beside me. His face, weathered by sun and wind, is cracked like the ground.

He darts a look at me. "You like our church?" he asks.

"Yes," I answer. "Very much. What do they mean, the two horses?"

"Oh," he says, "oh . . . ," drawing out the syllable so that it becomes musical prelude to story. "They are a symbol of our tribe. You'll find them down there at San Felipe, too. They say the horses are theirs, but they are not. We had them first." His eyes glint with laughter.

"What do the colors mean? Why is one black and the other brown?"

He shakes his head. "No meaning. Just what the painter feels. Every year, on the feast day of our pueblo, we paint them again. Different. You should come that day."

"I'd like to." It is the truth.

Again he looks at me, but it is as if he has donned a mask, become supplicant where before he was the possessor of dignity. "You want to buy jewelry? Very fine."

I'll not reward him for his change of demeanor. "No thanks. I'd just like to walk around."

"Ahhh." He understands. He opens the gate with a small bow, a courtly gesture. "Please. Look at the church. Go to the river. It is a good day to go there."

"Is it all right?" I am still the intruder, the tourist, bearing the history of change.

He nods and smiles, shattering the cracks upon his cheeks.

And then I am struck by a new thought. Even as I speak I know that it is not new, that I have been harboring it for a long time. "Does anyone have pottery?" I ask.

He tilts his head to one side like a crane and thinks. "Lucy may have some," he says finally. "She lives there. In the house near the *kiva*. You know the *kiva?*"

I follow his pointing finger. "Yes," I say. "I know. Thank you. I'll ask her." I bow to him, a repetition of his own. "First, I'll look in the church."

He drifts away like a brilliant shadow. He is there in the street, caught in sunlight, and then he vanishes as if he has taken flight like

109

the blackbirds that start from the trees when I enter the bowl of the plaza.

Inside the church it is cool, although hundreds of candles flicker in front of statues of the virgin and saints in carved niches. Colorful, over-decorated, this church is a repetition of all other missions except for the painted horses that curve above the lintel.

There is something of the toy about these churches, as if they are not taken seriously, used only for play, hung with ribbons, flowers, pictures in an excess of childish zeal.

"We here at Acoma did not become Christian until Nineteen Thirty-Eight," I was told there, and this despite the painted church, the mission school, the 200-year history of dedicated repression. If this is so — and I believe that it is — there is no reason to believe that Christianity has ever been accepted by these people. It is a game they play to safeguard ancient beliefs, placating the tide of white men who came, who still come, self-righteous, self-assured.

Beneath the façade of obedience runs a darker river. When the town gates are locked at sunset, does that river surface and run free? I believe that it does. I believe that it should.

Lucy's house is silent. No one comes in

answer to my knock. I stand in the deserted street and wonder what to do next.

"Pssst!"

The hiss comes from a small, round woman in moccasins and print dress. She gestures with her arm. "You want pottery?" she says in a whisper. "I have. You come."

I follow through her blue-painted door.

Inside, the walls are hung with remnants of carpet. All sizes, shapes, colors, nations are represented. Sears' finest, Mexican serapes, fragments of Persia, English tweed decidedly out of place amidst the opulence. The dirt floor retains the shapes of earth, but is covered with pieces of linoleum, green, yellow, red, again with no regard for aesthetics. Yet the effect is pleasing. I have walked into Ali Baba's cave; it gleams with jewels.

The woman turns, smiles, showing missing teeth, eyes that show humor. "Come," she says again. "I have fine pottery. Old. Sit. Please." She points to a couch that I reach by skirting a plaster garden statue of an old man and his burro. It stands waist-high, and, as I pass it, I wonder what she can show me, this person who lives with such outlandish creations.

She hums to herself, a strange, tuneless melody, and kneels before a cabinet, a key in her hand. "These were my grand-mother's," she says over her shoulder. "But my husband, he has a new pickup. We built a new house."

She shrugs, the timeless gesture of poverty. For pieces of metal, she is prepared to sacrifice her heritage.

Is it wrong to buy what she will show me? To indulge her and self? And then I forget my doubts. Jars, bowls, urns, a profusion of shapes, sizes, colors are taken down from the shelves. Some are painted with birds, others with vines and flowers springing life-like from the clay.

She is still humming. Perhaps it is a communion with the spirit of the grandmother, an asking for forgiveness. "Here," she says. "Touch. Hold."

She knows what she is doing. When I put my hands around the curved body of a flowered jar, I am lost, drawn into the coolness of clay, the spirit of the maker. No factory has or ever will replicate the touch of the human hand, the tiny irregularities, the almost invisible thumbprints of the artist. I feel that she and I have joined hands, as if we speak across time.

I put down the urn with sorrow. I don't have the money to pay her what these treasures are worth. Then I pick up a smaller bowl, painted in black and white geometrics. It fits between my palms as if I had wished it there. The shape is delicate, the black brush strokes sure, fine, delicate.

"This one," I say. "Maybe this one. How much would it be?"

She sits back on her heels. "One hundred dollars."

That, too, is more than I can afford. I look at the fragile thing and am shaken by the need for it, not as object but as creation of another's hands

"All I have is fifty," I say, ashamed.

She nods suddenly. "Good," she says. "You take." A heavy woman, she hoists herself to her feet and goes to sit on the couch. She beckons me to follow, and I do, putting the bowl down with care.

"You got glasses," she says. "Who's your eye doctor?"

I have forgotten my glasses, forgotten all the trappings of my life. I put up my fingers and touch the frames. "I'm from far away," I tell her. "My doctor is far away."

She smiles. "Not so far. Your heart is here."

And so it is. I smile back, and we sit in silence a while.

"What was your grandmother's name?" I ask.

"Rafoya," she says. "She was from Acoma. She died in Nineteen Twelve, I think."

"And your name?"

"Angelita. Yours?"

"Jane," I tell her struck by how out of place that sounds. "Jane."

She thinks a while. "Someday," she says, "you will find a better name."

I am not sure what she means. There are so many names we can call ourselves, so many truths in the sounds we carry as identification. I have always pictured myself as a bowl, perhaps this very one; as a repository of seeings, feelings, dreams; as bearer of children and words, dispenser of life.

I want to hug her, this short, plump woman in the orange and purple print, to know the solidity of her shape, and am surprised when she leans toward me and clasps my shoulders. "You come now," she says. "I will give you a loaf of my bread. You pay too much for the bowl, you know."

She wraps the loaf in brown paper, wraps the bowl as well. "Put it in your purse and go," she says. "And come back someday."

"I will," I tell her. "I will. Good luck to you."

When I have left the pueblo behind, I unwrap the bowl and place it beside me on

114

the seat where I can touch it, glance at it, treasure its beauty.

I race a line of thunderstorms down the center spine of New Mexico. Lightning crackles over the Jornada del Muerto, that infamous stretch of lava where nothing lives — eighty miles that brought terror to the hearts of those who crossed it.

The southern part of the state differs from the north. An extension of the Chihuahuan Desert, it is both violent and mystical. Vast stretches dotted with creosote recede into white sand, toward the twisted forms of volcanic mountains. Here are the great valleys that stretch north-south like fingers out of Mexico — the Animas, the San Simon, the Sulphur Springs, San Pedro, Santa Cruz, arteries of migrations defined by parallel chains of rock thrust, spewed, hurled heated and unpalatable out of the maw of an ancient earth.

This is the country of the Apache — of Mangus, Cochise, Geronimo — the country they fought for long after hope was gone.

"You are stronger than we. We have fought you so long as we had rifles and powder . . . give us weapons and turn us loose, we will fight you again. But we are worn out. We have no more heart. . . ."

Chief Gia-na-tah's words ring in my ears like the wind, a warrior's words torn from his heart.

Freedom has always been the crux of war. Tyranny has always been unbearable. And yet, what is freedom? It seems elusive, as much a mirage as the blue lakes of heat on the tableland of the desert. We are always bound, if not by one thing, then by another, by our bodies most of all.

Free of my past, it yet haunts me. Given time, I will be bound to words that spill out, clamoring to be noticed and written. I have chosen my own battlefield.

Tucson

All afternoon the clouds have been building, wisps at first, then the white torsos of thunderheads thrusting over the mountains. And now — the rain.

Here on the desert it comes as a gift, and it brings a lightness, a flurry of breaths and bloomings as if all must be done quickly; the buds must open, the branches drink and swell, the birds bathe in ephemeral puddles, frogs insure another generation.

It comes, and the air fills with fragrance. The touch of water releases a thousand scents, and I stand here lapping the wind, giving names to those elusive intangibles: damp mesquite like old fires; mimosa, feathery as flowers; sweet acacia; the novelty of water; the swelling of unseen, unnamed flowers under deadfalls, on the banks of flowing washes, their brilliant faces lifting for a night, for the blinding brevity of a day.

There is nothing sodden, nothing lush. Rain comes, is utilized, vanishes. Only the colors intensify, and the perfume. Green startles. The orange-red flowers of the barrel cactus flame. The fruit of the prickly pear swells, its color deepening to crimson and then purple. Even this fruit bears thorns and must be picked and peeled with tongs, although birds peck at it with delight.

It is the sparsity of growing things that gives the desert its magic. Each plant and tree, each mountain is separate, distinct in its own space. I am forced to be aware of shapes and shadings, individualities that elsewhere, in other climates, would be blurred or obliterated.

The palo verde is barren except in spring when it is covered by a mass of yellow flowers. Then the bees drink themselves tipsy. They drone and lift off slowly, as drugged by the thatch of yellow, perfumed hair as any human who stops, looks up, listens. Later what one sees will be the thicket of green twigs and branches, twining, clawing, synthesizing chlorophyll in place of leaves, and birds' nests, the completely round homes of verdin or wren, covered against the sun. And perhaps the clinging, paler green of mistletoe that takes up residence and eats of its host. But always it is the individual that startles, that is itself and no other.

Nothing can grow beneath creosote

bushes, and so they stand in rows like an orchard, the ground, barren, beneath. After a rain they give off a tangy scent reminiscent of the sea.

Earth here supports what is possible, each in its own space. On the surface, saguaro cacti do not crowd. They stand off from one another, each thrust distinctive, each arm naked in selfhood.

Even the higher forests have this sense of individual dignity. Light falls like rain between trees, sometimes stopping the heart with its purity.

With understanding comes respect. The desert has marked me. I walk carefully and guard against destruction, giving each thing its dignity, accepting my own, not without pain or regret for half a life lost.

Rain swirls through dark places, forms wordlessness into images, arouses discontent. What is around me, in me is changing second by second, calling with myriad voices, and, if I do not respond, do not accept the challenge, I will be small again, faceless, and in my insensitivity will surely die.

I wonder if it is true that Alfred Steiglitz, upon seeing Georgia O'Keeffe's early work, said: "At last, a woman on paper." If so, she had reason to be angry, to deny the sexuality of her work until she died.

She was not painting female sexuality as much as she was androgyny — the peculiar mingling of sexes as seen in the exposed hearts of flowers. She was celebrating the sensuality of union that shapes the essence of desert, of mesa country.

Earth's seasons and cycles, shapes and bloomings are female and have been so designated since man first understood the life process. "Mother Earth" we call it. "Life Giver." The Greeks gave us Demeter and Persephone who called forth flowers. Yet were it not for Pluto's demonic existence, the need for those flowers would not have arisen. Were it not for the male, the female gift would be no gift at all, and vice versa. So it is with earth and with art, with those who strain to understand themes and symbols.

In this country there is much that is harsh. The very bones of earth rip the thin soil and stand exposed. The desert in places is empty, blinding, and yet there is life. Flowers rear from cracks in the rock. In the sand are tracks of the living. And when the sun strikes fire from the mountains, when they burn at evening, changing shape and color like a garden, it is the mingling of extremes, the grace of opposites that excite.

Listening, looking, feeling with the underside of my skin, I come to awareness. It cannot be called knowledge, for it is scarcely conscious. It is feeling that illuminates the primal, and it is not distinguished by sex.

I believe that O'Keeffe knew what Steiglitz did not. She had found her way through and out of self and into the universal, and that is the mark of genius.

That she came to the West was no accident. She found truth in the starkness of mesas. She understood the struggle of shadows on the mountains, in the cañons, and she made these truths, these battles ours.

That I, too, have come is no accident. I dreamed this place before I saw it, spent years studying, making ready for the impact of desert and blinding sky. And yet, I was not ready. Dreams are intangible. This I hold in my hands.

What I do here will be mine. In no way can I put myself on equal footing with O'Keeffe or with anyone else save in the necessary honing of senses, the desire for silences so that thoughts may surface, bringing light to bear on the crux of earth, sky, and ultimately on the hearts of woman/man.

A Room of One's Own

Never have I had so much room — inside and out! Nor peace, time to sit thinking, letting the music that comes before words surface like fish in a pool, lazily in spirals, suddenly like swirls of light.

How valuable the world has become! Like a jewel box whose contents are infinite. There will never be enough time or silence to savor all of them, but I will cherish what I can.

In the mornings I awake before dawn and go out into the walled garden. There is no one to call me back, giving orders, no one to intrude on the voluptuousness of sunrise staining the sky saffron, orange, crimson, green, calling the mountains up from darkness.

When I go back inside, I make coffee, sit down at my desk, and write undisturbed. Words spill out like a flood through gates opened in me, gates once shut by circumstance.

In the afternoons I tend the garden, that tangible creation of my own hands. When I came, the yard was barren, an expanse of gravel without as much as a blade of grass. The sun beat mercilessly on the porch, left its heat in the stones long after dark.

A painter once remarked that it was hatred of blank spaces that drove her to work. Perhaps I am the same, filling white pages, imprinting my reflection on empty spaces. Whatever the reason, perhaps no more than a hunger for contact with soil, I dug and planted, watered and fed. Now an orange tree, a lime, and a lemon line the wall, oleanders shade the porch and perfume the air, a hanging basket trails shadows, and a red bird-of-paradise lures hummingbirds as jewel-like as the flowers from which they sip. Marigolds, zinnias, and herbs brighten what was an empty bed beside the house. They lift their faces like impudent children conceived in a burst of passion and as well loved.

In the evenings I call the dogs, my old setter Rascal and the shaggy Balto, mostly Newfoundland and given me by a friend as protection because I am living alone. We go down the alley behind the house to a patch of desert, a fascinating oasis in the middle of the city. No one else is ever there. It is a wild garden, home to scuttling quail, to rabbits, to lizards that in the twilight lie still, catching the last warmth from the sand, and to a coyote or two whose howls I can hear from the house late at night.

Sometimes I take a guidebook and learn the names and habits of plants I don't recognize, birds whose songs are unfamiliar — zygo-cactus, acacia, cactus wrens swinging in nests that are filled with broods of squabbling babies, grackles that chatter and flash iridescent wings.

Usually the sun sets while the dogs and I explore, the western horizon flaming like a lily that has entrapped the sun. Always then comes coolness, the sudden temperature drop of the desert. Branches sway, the last of the doves mourns, and elation sweeps me. I have done this! Broken out of my shell and hatched into other. Change is never impossible. No one need go down defeated, weeping tears of regret or defiance, blaming others. At beginning and end we have only the self and it is ours to discipline and nurture.

I remember a scene that took place on the day Glenn Boyer took me on a tour of some of the far places in what he has labeled "Wyatt Earp Country." We went over the top of the Chiricahua Mountains following the old outlaw trail, and down into Portal, Cave Creek, and Galeyville, sister boom town to Tombstone and rustler hide-out. Oddly enough, it was on that same trip where the voice urged me not to return. Perhaps what happened that day had more to do with my decision than I realized.

We had explored Onion Saddle, hiked along the sparkling water of Cave Creek, and marveled at the rock formations high above our heads. We had toured Galeyville, now privately owned and with hardly a trace of the original population. It was a bright but cool day, and by the time we reached Portal, we were ready for lunch.

The wood stove in the corner was radiating warmth, the service was quick, the hamburgers delicious. We talked about Earps and outlaws, about the abundance of grass in the San Simon Valley, about weather cycles, and, as we talked, I noticed the couple that sat at the next table. Their posture interested me. They reminded me of an old photograph, the kind that is dark and browning around the edges, the subjects, grandparents or uncles and aunts posed on the edges of chairs, uncomfortable with the whole procedure.

The woman, who had legs as thin as a crane's and white hair pulled into an untidy bun, sat with her hands folded in her lap. She looked at them, at her plate, not out of self-consciousness but out of what appeared to be timidity and a deadly boredom, as if, by focusing there, she was free to roam the world in her mind, relieved from the necessity to look at her husband who sat opposite her. He was as thin, as strained as she, but dominant in his bearing. He picked at his food forcefully, daring anyone to speak, to intrude on the importance of the moment, and his eyes bore malevolently into the crown of his wife's bent head.

It was a horrifying tableau of a marriage that had ceased to exist. What bound these two together was neither love nor hatred, but hopelessness, a community of habitual desperation. How many more such shattered beings existed? Worse, would I someday appear in this guise — a worn and frightened shadow?

I shivered as we pitched into our food with the appetites of those who have spent the day outdoors. We kept up our flow of conversation, and at some point I observed the old woman leaning back in her chair to listen.

I wanted to include her, but the old man's wicked stare kept me from doing so. Suddenly, however, he rose and without a word headed for the men's room. His wife picked at her plate for a moment as if she could eat only when alone. Then she turned around and faced us, her eyes alight.

"I've been listening to you talk about weather," she said, breathless, as if words were difficult for her. "The weather's so interesting. It reminds me of a book I read once. Saint-Exupéry, the man's name was." Then she sat, eyes darting from one to the other like a bird fearful of reprisal.

"It's a beautiful book," I said, surprised to have found a reader of literature in such an out-of-the-way spot. "*Wind, Sand and Stars.* I loved it, too."

Glenn leaned forward across the table, scenting a story, a bearing on history. "Are you from around here?" he asked.

She sat straighter, knees tightly together. "I was born here," she said. "In Nineteen and One. My daddy's ranch was here."

"I bet things have changed since then," he said.

She risked a smile. "My, yes! We had kerosene lamps. No conveniences. I walked miles to school, too, but it was fine. We had grass a while then, before the drought." She smiled again, more easily this time, her eyes half closed, remembering what?

The valley as it had been? An old love? One she still cherished in the place where her heart beat, shriveling?

"You loved it here," I said.

"My, yes!" she repeated. "But the weather, you know. All those dry years. It wasn't easy. We sold out. But I had it in my head all these years to come back. Just once more. We're from California now, but I wanted to see. . . ." Her voice fluttered and broke.

"It's still beautiful," I said gently. "The clouds, those mountains."

She didn't answer, simply stared at her hands folded again in her lap. Like a gargoyle her husband appeared and stood angrily beside his chair. She gathered her purse, wrapped her sandwich in her napkin. Then, clutching her worn white sweater tightly around her neck, she got up and followed him, taking small steps, watching the floor under her feet as if she no longer could trust the ground.

"Oh, dear God," I said.

And Glenn said: "Yes."

And then for a time we, too, were wordless, touched by the death of love, the fragility of living.

Horse Sense

"One thing you don't want to do is get an Appaloosa." Archie's words come back to me as I mount up on a wiry, leopard-spotted gelding I've been riding at a nearby stable. I've come so often and so faithfully that now I help wrangle dudes — taking tourists out on trail rides through the desert. All kinds of tourists, fat and thin, young and old, and dressed in everything from leotards to flowered shorts. Archie would have died at the sight. He would have argued about the horse that I love in spite of his warnings.

"Not a one doesn't have a problem. They're not a breed. They're just crazy, spotted horses."

Problems? I haven't had any, discounting the times he's run away with me down the wash, hair-raising minutes in which I relearned horsemanship in a hurry. No one but the greenest novice *falls off* a horse. Thrown off, yes. Falling off requires complicated and dangerous maneuvers done in a panic, and at least one horseman whom I know has a term for such a procedure. He calls it "candy-assing," a phrase I savor, chuckle over as I watch my dudes strung out behind me, arms and legs flailing like tadpoles.

Problems? Well, this horse shies at bedsprings. When I mention this, people look at me strangely. Where am I riding, anyway?

The unfortunate fact is that the desert, like the ocean, has become the dumping ground of mankind. Unlike the ocean, however, the detritus does not sink and disappear but lingers where left, refusing to rot or rust in the dry air.

Even so, how many of these things can there be? After all, not everyone rushes to the desert to dispose of their household goods. In an area of fifteen square miles I have come across at least twenty sets of springs and attendant mattresses, ten couches, and innumerable chairs and car seats, not to mention stoves, refrigerators, the shells of dismantled automobiles, and once, in ponderous Victorian splendor, a complete wooden bed with a high, carved headboard. It stood at the edge of the trail beneath a twisted mesquite, abandoned and out of place.

I looked at it a long time, there being no springs in sight to frighten the horse, and I debated going for a truck to haul it home. I did not. Two days later it was gone, prey, perhaps, to another stealthy dumper who discarded and then helped himself to a treasure, for that it certainly was. It is the only treasure I have ever found in the desert, and I worry about it. Who left it and why? It was surely valuable and, therefore, to find it there must mean it had a painful history. Perhaps too many had died in it, or suffered, and so it was smuggled out of a house and left to its fate.

This is easier to understand than out and out disregard for the character and beauty of the land. We live in cities with regular refuse hauling. To discard, we have only to dismantle and leave at the curb or place in a dumpster. The ease with which this is done cannot compare to the labor of loading a truck, driving several miles over non-existent roads, and unloading all again. So where is the rationale? It cannot be laziness. Can it be some twisted notion of neatness? Does out of sight equate with out of mind?

But these discards are not out of my sight, nor of those others who hike and ride in the supposed wilderness. The bedsprings are there, coiled and lurking, distressing a horse that leaps in the air at the very hint of such a predator, his eyes bulging, his tail high, and me holding for dear life and wishing I could catch the litter bugs in the act. That must happen in the dark of night, however. The doers must know that debasement is wrong and wind their way in secret, fearful of discovery.

Yet, given the present-day state of visual and plastic art, perhaps they do not consider what they do defacement but rather as enhancement. Picture these modern Michelangelos brandishing scraggly mops, vacuum cleaners, the bent legs of broken grills and kitchen tables, artists all, depositing here and there a statement. Henry Moore carved doughnuts. Joe Doakes, dumpster extraordinaire, strings stoves out like boxcars. Jackson Pollock shot bullets of paint, dribbled sand on his canvases. Jaime Garcia wrings bedsprings into bundles; the sand is his canvas. Andy Warhol made monuments of cans and movie stars. Johnny Kowalsky, hopping among thorns like a jack rabbit, hangs cans from twigs, stacks newspapers at random.

Richard Serra, the removal of whose "Tilted Arc," a wall stretched across a New York City plaza, was the subject of a battle in Federal Court, has also decorated the landscape willy-nilly. The result, as I recall, is no more pleasing than these mounds of discards. The pomposity of the statement is the same. Man's simplest leavings, conscious or otherwise, are as valid as those of nature, the equal of foliage and hills.

There is no immediate solution to the dilemma and will not be until our wild places have become so rare that they, too, will be viewed as works of art, from behind glass and miles of rope barriers.

For the moment, we can no longer differentiate between creation and disorder. We have passed out of the realm of taste and have left discernment to the horse.

Rancho Milagro

The San Pedro Valley

Inevitably the city palls. I long for earth, chafe at the restraints of streets, traffic, the neighbor's uninterrupted television game shows which stream over the wall and enlist me as unwilling voyeur. It is not enough to look at mountains, to ride the desert. I need to be in and upon them, to open my door and be one with the flowing.

The city holds the heat until nearly sunrise. Awake in the night I remember isolated scenes from a painful marriage. Wounds of the spirit heal slowly, pucker into scars that retain the ability to hurt. I mourn for the lost years, the unproductive years made possible by my own innocence, and I curl into myself seeking comfort. Even my wild garden has vanished, prey to developers' greed.

Because I had been to a writers' conference, I skipped my nightly walks for several weeks. And then I had a visitor who fell in love with the desert and who wanted to walk there.

We called the dogs who came, ears up, eyes shining, looking forward to their run.

"It's beautiful," I said. "Wait till you see." And we set off down the alley.

But at the end, where once it had opened on trees, trails, the wings of birds, it opened now on a wasteland. Nothing remained of the haunting beauty that had been there a short while before. The desert had been leveled. The earth-moving equipment stood parked where the small wash had run, where the dogs had splashed, and the birds gone to drink. There were no birds. There was only a great and final silence.

The dogs sat down suddenly as if they had been struck and looked at me. And I stood staring, feeling the first stirrings of violation as if it were my body that had been ripped apart, separated from life.

I remember that I put out my hands feeling for solidarity, for branches, thorns, anything at all that would give purchase on the slipping past of what I had taken for granted. And then I began to curse, words being all that remained to me.

Now I wonder where the rape will end? And how? And who will find the courage to say — "Enough!" — to those who put up a house a day on the emptiness, who are compelled to fill the void that they have made, who have never walked at sunset and heard the voices of the land, loved the weaving of growing things.

I remember Archie who watched the approach of trailer parks, the inundation of campers and RVs with dread. "Big business lining its pockets," he'd said as he often did. "It's all changed. All the mystery is gone."

I know what he felt. I know the frustration, the bitterness that catches in the throat, the pain of loss. Rape is not confined to the body. There is rape of the heart, the spirit, the intangible holdings of the soul. And its consequences multiply.

When we all, every one of us, are confined in our houses, when we finally look out and see nothing but squares, rectangles, walls in endless repetition, what will we feel then?

Will future generations be so deaf, so blind, so hemmed in by screens, headsets, concrete that the earth on which they stand makes no difference to them?

Will someone look out and say: "I have been violated. My rights have been taken. A part of me has been destroyed."

Or will we all have been raped too much, too long to care?

Just as these questions rise to a shouting, as the need to escape the city becomes necessity, I find a ranch to rent, a place of tall grasses and the sweep of plain. Seven mountain ranges dominate the horizon: the forested Huachucas to the west; the Mustang Hills and the Whetstones to the northwest; the pink-shouldered Dragoons and the dark Tombstone Hills to the northeast; the Mules to the east; and, south, over the border in Mexico, the San José Mountains with striated green and dun flanks that turn gold at sunset. Behind them, in diminishing strata of purple, are other ranges whose names I do not know, am not sure I want to know. They are far away in a strange country, the border of which is almost at my door. It is enough that they are there, sharp in the morning light, cloud-like at twilight. Someday, perhaps, I shall explore them. For now, this place, my place, the writing I must do is enough.

Oddly, it is not twenty miles from that spot where I stopped one evening, secure in the hand of God. So I call it Rancho Milagro. Miracle Ranch. And that it is.

Ruby

If there is a clock here, or the passing of time, it is noticeable only in the blooming of plants, the shifting of sky from the cloudless burning of May and June to the thunderheads of the summer rainy season.

I awake to a shimmer of light, a gentle apology before the ferocity of noon. Dawn comes early, the sky over the Mules turning pearl gray, then yellow, then the piercing coral of a spiral shell. In the meadows the larks sing, music so sweet the human throat constricts in longing, and even the mockingbird, he of the hundred trills and variations, turns silent in deference. His silence is a rarity. Often in the night he wakes and sings from his nest in the honeysuckle as if in sleep he dreams melodies and, waking, practices, his notes cascading like a stream over the leaves, into the still air. From my bed I applaud him, magician, concertmaster, winged flute.

Here is the essence of timelessness. Earth goes on as it always has, to its own rhythms that we city-dwellers have forgotten. Wind lifts the leaves, birds swoop and sing, mate, and nest; the mountains change color as the sky changes color, now purple, now a glowing rose.

It was not so long ago that we, all of us, lived close to nature, rising with the sun, sleeping when night fell, neither knowing that time was running forward, nor caring that we were behind in the race. Even today much of the world's population lives in such a way, making their own time regardless of date lines, zones, laws, and politics, and are happier for it.

So I have ceased to count days or hours. I live instead by the needs of animals, the ripening of fruit. There is an orchard here, a grape arbor, and chickens, dogs, cats, and two spotted horses that graze in the fields, dappled rumps blending with the grasses, the moving flowers. There is Jefe, my Appaloosa, and Segundo — Chief and his Second. Jefe is small, fiery, quick as a cat. Segundo is big and dark with the placidity of all large creatures that do not find it necessary to fight for a place in the order of things. They are opposites and friends, and they are my friends, too.

There is also a caretaker, Floyd and his wife Ruby. Or there was a wife, a small, broken-faced woman with dyed red hair and a yearning for drink who tended the strawberries, the roses, the trees, who did interminable washings in the old machine, hanging the clothes and leaving them on the line, often overnight, a moving, rag-tag quilt.

It was Ruby who fed the chickens and gathered the eggs — brown, white, pale green. Ruby who watched the sun rise from her porch steps, a tiny figure in a tattered, red chenille bathrobe, her sunken profile sharpening as the light intensified.

It was Ruby who questioned me when I came. "Do you like to garden? Do you like to can? Oh, we'll have lots to do come summer." And she led me into her kitchen to show me her collection of seed packets: radishes, peas, Swiss chard, three kinds of tomatoes, lettuce, celery, carrots. Together we planned where the gardens would be, and I gave her a present of a packet of purple coneflowers, those lovely liftings from the prairie dry lands. I drank a beer with her that day, and watched her eyes twinkling over the rim of the can.

I grew used to her boisterous laugh, to the way her speech slowed down and slurred as the day lengthened, to the sight of her wrapped in a crocheted cape of many colors, driving off with Floyd on evenings when they had money to spend, shopping to do, beer to drink.

Removed from me though she was by birth, education, circumstance, she was a woman, and there was a bond between us, unspoken, undefined, a softness as we knelt and turned the earth and talked of planting. This was how friendships were formed on the historical frontier between women of vast differences, even between white women and red. Women whose purposes were similar and who, in a world of men, spoke of the small acts, the artistry of nurturing, and in so doing nurtured themselves.

Yet, then as now, the West had high alcoholism and suicide rates. Women then and now hanged themselves in barns. Like Mattie Earp, they drank and took overdoses of drugs, or blotted out the world with a bullet. Why? It has to do with isolation as much as with despair. In the past, women were often left to cope with hunger, drought, Indians, wolves, plagues of grasshoppers, the ordeal of childbirth, often with a flock of other children at the bedside. Economic necessity stranded them, then as now, on prairie, mountain, desert, and many succumbed to loneliness, to never-ending labor, to the sheer weight of survival without hope of change.

Why Ruby chose to end her life one night shortly after my arrival cannot be explained, least of all by Floyd who found her, gun in hand, the next morning. Neither he nor I heard the shot, but sound is tricky here. The wind warps it. Trees and buildings distort and throw echoes. So we did not hear, and could not have helped if we had.

I am no stranger to suicide, yet it always leaves me troubled, angered, and with a feeling of helplessness. In my life as a teacher at a women's college, I had several students who, burdened beyond their strength and years, made the attempt. Some of them succeeded. Always I felt the futility of the act and berated myself for not having recognized the signs of despair.

"Nothing is so bad that it can't be changed," I would tell my students. "Everything passes. If you need to talk, come to me. Call me at home. Any time. Please." I would tell them to stop looking inward and look out, to reach for another person, even if only for a moment. Earth goes on, its beauty continues for us to partake of. To choose to deprive ourselves of opportunity, even of the opportunity for pain, is sinful.

Had I known what Ruby was planning, I would have taken her hand, walked with her in the garden, planted seeds, searched for words, and hoped they were the right ones.

But I did not, and she is gone. Now the yuccas are blooming, forests of waxen tree-flowers so heavy the stalks bend, sometimes falling but more often remaining at an angle season after season, the dried bells nests for birds, refuge for insects.

The ocotillo, skittering tongues of fire, have bloomed, and now the sunflowers come. Now figs appear on the branch, lime green swellings like small hot air balloons. And the summer rains threaten, thunderheads pushing up over the mountains, casting shadows, great purple flowers on their flanks.

Now the garden I planted stirs. The corn is up, and the zucchini. The tomato plants lift, the peppers begin to bloom in earnest. Life quivers everywhere, runs through the grass like prairie fire, and those of us who are here rejoice, put out our tongues and taste the wind. Put out our arms and hold the mountains close.

Life is a gift we must not spurn or give back before time, a rich and precious tapestry to which we must add our own fragments, awkward though they may be.

While I did not know Ruby long or well enough to miss her, still I do. And sometimes, early in the morning, I think I see her small person on the steps or stooped over the strawberries, shaded by apple leaves, touched by sky.

The Cutting Edge

Time then is reckoned here by the sun, the season, the cycles of birthing.

Each morning the horses appear at the fence, heads up, ears alert, eager for oats after a night of grazing. The dogs wake, stretch, sniff the ground for news of what has passed through during the night. Often it will be javelinas, small wild pigs whose hoofs I can sometimes hear, light and swift, in the yard.

Foals are born, and young calves appear in the fields beside the stolid warmth of their mothers. Roundup time comes again, a part of the cycle, and, when my friend Alicia invites me to help her cousin on a roundup, I accept eagerly. I have ridden for him several times and enjoyed the new terrain, the feel of a good horse, the warmth of Lily's kitchen, the table piled high with Mexican food.

Today we have a stiff wind at our backs and fine particles of dust in the air. The way to the corrals seems twice as long, the cows skittish and overly watchful.

We separate the calves, driving them into a pen, and the mothers bawl and surge outside, and rush the gate with a clatter of hoofs and horns. Robert heels the calves; I throw them, grabbing diagonal legs. They go down easily. Then Beto ties them securely with piggin' strings — narrow strips of rawhide wrapped around small feet. When we have finished, thirty calves lie on their sides bawling in terror

"You want to cut one?" The way Robert says it, it is almost a dare, and since my tomboy days I've never backed away from one. Nevertheless, at this moment I draw a breath and think. Do I really want to castrate a calf? More to the point, can I?

I look at Robert. He is dark, compact, proud, every inch the *vaquero,* born to this way of life as I was not. I have learned. I have ridden roundups, driven cattle, stayed on bucking horses, thrown and tied my share of calves. But cut one? Never!

He does not look away. I read in his eyes the chance he is offering. My baptism of blood. Opportunity to leave the epithet "dude" behind once and for all. In addition, I see a glint of humor, the amusement of the chauvinist male faced with feminine vapors. Am I coward, or do I truly belong here in the wind, dust, cacophony of cows bawling

146

their lungs out? Am I simply playing cowboy, or am I the real thing?

I look at Alicia. Under the broad brim of her hat, her face is chalk white. "Are you?" I ask, hoping for company.

She shakes her head. "No way," she says. "Not me."

She, of course, has no need to prove herself. She belongs. Her family has been here for centuries, part and parcel of a land, a way of life. But her fright pushes me forward.

"All right," I say, gritting my teeth. "Tell me what to do."

Robert nods, a short, sharp motion of his head. "Come." He leads me among the calves. Some are still crying, throwing back their heads and rolling up their eyes. Others seem stunned and lie quiet, pink tongues lolling.

From beyond the gate a spindly-legged brindle cow, mostly Brahma from the look of her, tosses her horns. "Go on, mama," I yell. She is a pusher, a crowder of the fence, the leading wedge in a sea of disturbance.

"Never mind. Moro will watch her." Robert indicates his gray horse that stands guard, reaching over occasionally to nip the crowding mothers.

"We'll do this one." He kneels beside a

white calf that is lying still.

Beto the *vaquero*, who speaks no English and who rides a feisty black Appaloosa as if he has sprouted from its back, kneels, too. Then he hands me his knife. It is thin-bladed and razor-sharp. I heft it in my hand. Test it with my thumb in a gesture I haven't used since childhood games of mumblety peg. Beto's dark eyes gleam with the same humor I saw in Robert's. He, too, has his doubts about the American *señora* with her white hands and innocent face who comes now and again to drive cows.

I steel myself, try to blot out fear, the possibility of squeamishness. There is a job to be done. The cutting of the hide, the removal of testicles that slide out from the sack, slick and gleaming, so slippery that I have to go after them several times, probing with steady fingers. I cut. Then cut again. The job is done. Robert, smiling now with approval, stretches out a bloody hand and shakes mine. Hard.

It is over before I had time to think or feel. It was an act performed. It is what is done, what has been done on ranches for centuries. I stand in the glare of the noon sun blinking, rubbing my hands together. They are sticky with blood. "Who am I?" I ask myself. "Who?"

How did I, the lady from the East, perform such an act without hesitation or fainting? I step outside myself and see a figure standing proudly in the dust, the wind. My senses know. My hands. The smell of it all is in me, the feel and taste of roundup. The sun, the stench of branding, the suddenness of blood.

We do what we have to do, we men and women. In this I am no different from thousands, those who came before me and those who will come after. I am a link in a chain and a strong one. I will not break.

Drought

Years ago I used to do an imitation of two ranchers meeting. Without preamble one would say: "We had five-tenths of an inch up our way yesterday." And the other would shake his head, half congratulation, half commiseration. "Shoot!" he'd say. "Our wash went to runnin' with what we got. And the weatherman says more's on the way." Then they'd square their hats and talk about grass, feed, cattle prices, and the year it really rained before taking leave of one another.

Then I'd tell about the rain-maker Archie saw in his youth — a real conjure-man with pinwheels, smoke-sticks, and bells — who set himself up on a hill where he prayed, threatened, cajoled the heavens while lost in a cloud of his own making. The way Archie told it, something worked, or the rain-maker chose his time well. The rains came. The grass was saved. Cattle grew fat and were shipped to market.

This year I learn the truth of what used to be a joke. Without rain, plants and animals die. It's that simple. Here, in the Southwest, water is vital for survival. I realize this as I pump it onto the grape vines, the fruit trees, the vegetables; as I fill and refill the horses' troughs in the corrals, the dogs' dishes scattered in shady places; as hot, dusty, desiccated I stand under the shower with my face in the spray. I have begun to long for the ocean that I haven't thought about in years. I replay scenes of my childhood by the sea, remembering the greenness of water, the hiss of foam at tide line, the shock of the cold as I dived in. I remember Oyster River and the bridge over the tidal inlet where the shadows were dark and cool, and where I played for hours hypnotized by the motion of reeds and grass in the flow of the river.

While I dream, the pasture turns to broom straw. Day after day the sun rises, burns from a cloudless sky, descends in a bath of flame. With a twinge of irony, I hear myself talking on the phone. "You get any rain over there?" In my voice is both hope and the readiness to curse if the answer comes back: "Yes."

The old-timers, those readers of signs and purveyors of doom who have lived through flood and drought and who delight in tainted recollection, say: "We had rain in May. That means a dry summer. All we'll get is lightnin' and plenty of it. Forest fires, too."

Doggedly then, without much hope, I go on setting up sprinklers, getting chores done at sunup and sunset when it is cool, when the sun cannot burn my eyes, pierce through my clothes, tan me like a piece of saddle leather.

I discover the necessity of *siesta*. There is nothing else to do from noon to three, and, having been up and working since five, sleep is a necessity. With the drop of the sun, the temperature drops. The horses come in. Larks swoop and sing, flashing white tail feathers. The dogs wake from torpor and go off full speed through the fields chasing the large jack rabbits that likewise awake toward evening.

And to the south the mountains begin to burn as if from within, their smooth flanks turning cinnabar, rose-red shot with gold like a piece of silk I found in a shop and held and marveled over. The radiance lasts perhaps an hour, never long enough. When it has gone, when the fire has faded and the slopes lie in the blue of evening, I can never quite recall the fiery beauty although I have lapped the colors with my eyes, gone out with that part of me that hungers for the blessings of earth.

But beauty lies in the very swiftness with which earth gives to us. Left to itself, nature is never wrong, never distorted. Its rituals are marked by rightness; in its heart is justice, an unerring sense of past, present, future. And beneath all of this is a violence sensed rather than seen, the feel of an implacable will.

Buzzards cluster on the water tank at noon, huge birds, big as turkeys. They come to drink after feasting on the putrid carcass of a dead horse in a nearby pasture. The sun carves the bones that are fast settling into dry ground. The birds, the coyotes feed. This is the violence of inherent truth, as in the sun striking rock, triggering fires in the forest, and I respond to it with an instinct that accepts these acts as cleansing. At times like these I am kin to John Muir who loved the violence of mountains, who ran toward storms and rock falls waving his arms in ecstasy, convinced of the presence of God.

The Mexican tradition says that the summer rains begin on June 24th, the Feast Day of San Juan. If, legend goes, it does not rain that day, there will be no rainy season at all.

It is now past mid-July, and we are waiting. I have had one grass fire, an ominous, galloping wall of orange that charred several acres of pasture and would have ruined more had not my neighbor leaped onto his tractor, smashed down my fence, and plowed a break of twenty feet in a circle around the flames.

No one has anything good to say about this man. No one, in fact, speaks to him at all. Yet when the fire was out and we stood, face-to-face in the plowed earth, I saw a young, intelligent person, sturdy and straightforward, who was apologizing for driving through my fence.

That struck me as ludicrous. Of what use is a fence without the grass and animals it protects? A hundred acres, a thousand, could have gone without his quick action, and I said so.

He was unmoved by my gratitude. "I'll fix it in the morning," he said. "You got any stock out?"

I'd driven the horses to the barn at the first sight of black smoke. "No," I said, and tried again to thank him. But he was already walking away, having, I suppose, spoken more than he was used to.

I stood a minute in the ashes, holding gratitude like a live coal. What to do with thanks refused?

In the ditches sunflowers bloom, the small, wild ones with saucy faces; by night the datura raises poisoned goblets. Poison or not, these are splendid flowers, often six inches high, a pure white streaked with lavender and, deep inside, a darker heart. The yuccas bear fruit, some falling down completely under the weight of the pale green shells, and here and there a century plant, having gathered its strength, puts out arms and flowers that reach toward the sky.

Young mockingbirds are leaving the nests. For a week the yard is cluttered with wings, rent with chatter as they begin to fly amidst parental concern, watched over by the ranch cats with their gleaming eyes. Then the adults mate again. They plummet through the leaves flashing white-spotted wings, sing early, late, constantly. On the night of the full moon I am kept awake by the splashing of song, the flood of silver light.

This is like no moonlight I have ever seen. It flows like a river, floods the valley, dances over grasses in a pouring out that is almost tactile. It presses gently upon me. I raise my face to it, scoop it in my hands, drink it like water, and, when at last I return to bed, it is there at the window so bright that it dazzles even behind closed lids.

The old tales of moon madness cannot be wrong, for truly there is madness upon me, a joy so that I will not, cannot sleep but lie awake listening to the night's music.

In the fields the horses are also awake. Jefe runs the fence, neighing at the neighbor's mares. When I get up again, I see him, curved, arched, creature of myth, his spotted rump gleaming like a sky splashed with stars. In his heart, in the heated core of him, he is stallion tonight, and he cries his desire again and again, fruitless though it may be, touched as he is by lunacy, his hoofs striking fire from the ground.

Rain

Suddenly one morning the sky is filled with clouds. I have become so used to the blue bowl that stretches overhead brassy with heat, to mountains unadulterated by shade, that I stand a long time watching new shadows paint the stones, define cañons with color and a new depth.

"Nothin' in them," the man at the feed store tells me about these clouds. "They're just itty-bitty. We need big ones and a wind shift first."

"Pray for the whole nine yards," Ty, the farrier, says, spitting tobacco juice and uttering his favorite statement. "The old-timers can be wrong."

Somewhere in Mexico it is raining, therefore it must rain here sooner or later. I continue watering the tomatoes and the corn, fighting grasshoppers that have discovered the roses, but there is a lightness in me, hope where hope had been worn to a nub, and with this a new ability to see.

I do not, for instance, have it in my heart to kill the grasshoppers. They are unlike any

I have ever seen, painted jewels blazing with color, lacquered insects the size of brooches, a perfect pattern of pale green, scarlet, yellow, blue brush strokes.

I know I would feel differently if a cloud of them descended; if they ate everything in sight including the clothes on the line; if they fouled the water and left me without crops and penniless as happened numerous times to homesteaders in the last century. I know how I would feel if they landed in my hair or crawled on my face chewing and spitting and dragging jointed legs. But they do not, nor do they come in uncontrollable numbers. Instead I find one here, one there, and am always drawn to observe, marveling at bodies so brilliantly camouflaged, so well designed for living.

Day by day clouds build. I can see rain far to the south, and lightning. Day by day I study the sky, watch the wind, and then one morning the sun rises behind a cloud the color of ox blood, pushing its way above the Mule Mountains as if through a solid body before splitting into fragments as shaggy as chrysanthemum petals. There is thunder in the distance, and for the first time the scent of water in the air. It is distinct in this dry land, cool and green like perfume.

The leaves turn belly-up; flies begin to

bite; the horses swish their tails and stomp frenetically. On my way to the post office a red racer flashes across the road, his body whip-like, a nearly translucent uncoiling of red. Farther on, a green Mojave rattler lifts his lethal head from the roadside dust. From far back in memory I dredge up old maxims: "Snakes crawl before rain." "Flies bite." "When the leaves turn up, it'll rain." "Red sun at morning." Like the old-timers, I have begun to read signs, not knowing if there is truth in them. "Plant root crops in the dark of the moon," Archie used to say, and he spent an entire afternoon explaining the signs of the Almanac, and how you never castrated animals when the signs were in the heart, only in the feet or legs. Who am I to disbelieve the old ways?

From the post office I continue east into town, passing through the arid plain where the Mule Mountains end — or begin — a jumble of thrust rock and ocotillo-covered outcroppings.

On the way home, the entire southern end of the San Pedro Valley lies spread before me, a palette of desert colors — yellow grass, red earth, the green of cottonwood trees following the windings of the river and beyond, anchored in space, mountains covered by a dancing veil of rain.

It is this that the West gives to us; this sense of distance and perspective, the ability to view acts of nature — and of man — in entirety. Who, locked in a city, has witnessed a storm from a distance of fifty miles, has watched the silver ribbon move down and across rock face and desert, and in that watching become part of a greater whole? Who can say — "I have seen the rain." — and mean a reaching out of self, a becoming of cloud and water, the shiver of dry earth?

I drive forward to meet it, open the window to catch the scent and the taste. Now I am in the fringes of storm. Small drops spatter the windshield, becoming larger and more frequent as I drive beneath opening clouds into the storm's heart. In the core of it, wind rocks the car, the shining veil becomes an opaque curtain of water through which I force my way. It is a gully-rolling, hen-drowning rain, the "whole nine yards." It fills the washes and carves the soft red stone banks of the draw with its rush of water, the moving branches of uprooted trees.

Every year a few of the innocent are drowned by a storm such as this, when depressions in the desert turn to cauldrons, dips in the road to dark torrents. Fortunately I have no such washes to cross, so I keep on, stirred by a sense of combat, re-membering Muir again, his delight in the power of storm as if he were tossed in God's hands.

Like a seed that has lain dormant, I feel myself stir, lift like a stem. In this Western space I have found room to grow, reason to flower. In the past, in the present, there were many who, faced with such immensity, quailed, turned inward, even died, but I will not die so easily.

By the time I reach the narrow dirt road to the home ranch, the storm has passed. A rainbow, miles high, arches from one mountain range to another, a fountain of pure color across blue sky. As I pass beneath, I think that, despite drought and violence and the slicing edge between beauty and despair, I would not trade places with anyone else on earth.

Pas de Deux

In the west garden, yellow butterflies are dancing, coming together, then fluttering apart and drifting through the trees like small, winged leaves.

Watching, I think about miracles, an apt subject for a place named Rancho Milagro. Do miracles happen by divine intervention, or do we, by our actions, our words, restructure the shape of the world, change the course of lives.

What has happened to me seems part miracle, and part of a flowing I cannot discern. Here, on this isolated ranch, I have become other — no stranger to myself but simply that woman who had been hiding within, shielding herself from harm. She and I have, it seems, exchanged places. Now she is the one who speaks and speaks freely without fear of reprisal. What remains of the self that clung so doggedly to existence is faith, hope, and a blossoming but totally unexpected happiness.

Is there such a thing as destiny, or do we make our own? In the garden, under the mulberry trees, the butterflies continue with their dance. Seek, mate, lay eggs, and die. . . . This is the destiny of most living things, and there are moths that fly a thousand miles to find their mates. Here, now, almost a continent away from what was, once, familiar, my own flight has changed the entire course of my life.

Love comes to us — or it does not. But when it does, it comes as a gift, a miracle that cannot quite be comprehended, but for which we must give thanks. For the first time in my life, I am deeply and passionately in love with no holding back.

As I have discovered, love between adults withholds nothing. There is no part of me that must be hidden away or protected. I have no secrets, nor does he.

Glenn, who, as he admits, enjoys what he calls "Jane watching," asks: "Where have you gone?"

I answer. "Out dancing with the butterflies. I remember the day I met you . . . at the writer's conference in Silver City. I looked at you, and the ground moved under my feet, and I thought *this man will never hurt me.* I didn't know what I meant then. It's taken me years to understand."

He puts his hands on my shoulders. They are warm, kind hands that I have seen nurturing newborn kittens, calming a frightened horse. "I'll try never to hurt you," he says.

"Me, too," I say, and under my skin my bones shift like tectonic plates. Then: "Do you believe in miracles?"

"In this one I do."

We have both been used enough, hurt enough by life and by previous bad marriages, but we are the survivors, and unlike the moths, the butterflies, we have "world enough and time."

Part Three

Mountain Time
The San Simon Valley
1988–2000

Home

On this evening that is as still, as silent as the first night of Creation, I give thanks for the vision that brought me to these mountains, this valley that I now call home, and to a new and happy marriage that is all that marriage and love should be.

In the whole of the velvet evening, nothing moves but four horses released from their stalls after their evening feed and heading out to pasture — one chestnut, one paint, one bay, and my old Appaloosa, Jefe, in *bas relief* against the last light on the Peloncillo Mountains.

There is nothing as beautiful as horses — curves, angles, pointed ears, bodies designed for speed and endurance. I watch them a long time, listen to hoofs striking stone, marvel at the perfection of form, the evolution of eohippus into these most striking of creatures making their way out into pasture, into semi-wildness, where the mountains themselves take on the shape and color of animals — taupe, fawn, and appearing almost tangible.

Sometimes I feel that I can gather these mountains in the palms of my hands and know the texture of grasses, the silk of sand and smoothness of rock, the ethereal grace of dancing poppies. And in those moments I become all things; in those flashes of intuitive unity, knowledge of the world comes to me, and it is blessed.

It was the mountains, Peloncillos and Chiricahuas, that more than anything wove the spell that prompted Glenn and me to buy the original house and forty acres. The first fall we were here, I stood in awe of those mountains, and of the clouds of migrating Monarch butterflies that day after day swept down the valley — an orange and black tidal wave, a kaleidoscope of ever-changing patterns.

Butterflies were everywhere — sleeping on purple asters, sipping from the yellow daisies and the painted galliardias — a stream of minute, jeweled insects on their way to a mountain in Mexico. They dazzled my eyes, made harmony in ears attuned to the small singings of earth, and broke my heart with their fragile courage.

Standing over all were the Chiricahuas, their eastern face unfamiliar to me then but bearing, in their rock slopes and scalloped contours, the same magic that I had found years before on the western side.

Someone, I don't know who, has called these mountains "Sky Islands," a misnomer. They are not islands but fortresses — barriers, guardians of secrets we have yet to learn. And there they stand, in our back yard, rising from the valley floor without preamble or apology, miles-high thrustings of pink rock, mesquite-shrouded slopes, pine-shaded peaks cut by cañons and draws, the thin thread of a road that crawls to what is known as Rustler Park at the top of the mountain, and then descends in dizzying spirals.

These are mountains that beckon and dominate, that invite and then shroud themselves from we who ride and hike the hidden passages.

"Come," they say.

And then: "Leave us to ourselves."

It is my belief that in the night, when the only light is that of the stars and a sickle moon, these mountains shift, re-arrange themselves, murmur unheard by humans, laugh, and perhaps even dance, releasing a shower of stones.

We find the stones every morning, on top of sand, in the corral, where the day before there was only dirt. I know that the mountains speak, that the valley trembles with their weight. I know, but cannot yet hear.

Water Music

The vermillion flycatcher swoops down from his perch on a cottonwood branch and skims the surface of the pond. For one brilliant moment he is reflected on the surface, a flash of red like no other, a meteor shattering stillness. Then he returns to his branch, ruffling the crest that has given him his Latin name: *Pyrocephalus rubinis* — "firehead."

It is morning, and I am in what has become my favorite thinking place — beside the pond Glenn and I put in shortly after moving here.

It has been fourteen years since we bought the small house set in the midst of overgrazed scrub land, the vegetation characteristic of the high desert with its (supposed) eighteen inches of rain a year. Yard and pasture were dotted with mesquite and catclaw, yucca and bunch grass, with here and there, in isolated patches, a few stands of the grama grass that once made this ideal cattle country.

Although "desolate," had been the reaction of other prospective buyers, the isolation, the primitive beauty was precisely what we had been searching for.

"Paradise!" we said, looking east across the San Simon valley at the rounded brown backs of the Peloncillos and west to the Chiricahuas.

Both of us were imagining our horses grazing on our own pasture, long rides into the twisting and secretive cañons that cut through both chains of mountains, and we had wanted a place of our own in which to write and ride without interference. In this valley, we found it.

Being gardeners, we began immediately to improve on our paradise, planting Arizona cypress as a windbreak, Russian olive for the lemony scent of the blossoms, mulberries and chinaberries for quick shade, and, one spring, the thirty-foot tops off a neighbor's cottonwoods, bare poles that I looked upon with suspicion. All those holes dug for a bunch of unwieldy logs that would probably end up as firewood.

"Just wait," Glenn said. "They'll grow."

Much to my astonishment, the poles leafed out, grew branches, put down roots. Today they are trees, real ones fifty feet high, and, with the rest, have become home to every bird in the guidebook.

As in all desert places, however, the necessary ingredient for an oasis is water. With the digging of the pond — that turned out to be much larger than we'd planned due to the front-end loader's operator who wanted to dig straight to China — came all the creatures of earth and air. We have created a lifesaver in a country that, these past few years, has been drought-stricken.

From the bank where I sit, I once watched a badger, with beautifully marked face and what can only be called "an attitude," make his way back to his burrow after drinking his fill.

This is the place where once again I have heard the rarest of all music — the song of the porcupine — always in the deepest time of night, always when fall is verging into winter.

Now I stare into the depths of water, watching at least a hundred bullfrogs — some floating motionless on the surface, some hanging vertical, their webbed feet absurdly like a skin diver's flippers, others crouched on the muddy banks, but all observing me with what appears to be at least as much interest as I have in them.

The grunts, squeaks, growls, and croakings these fellows emit are reminiscent of a grade school orchestra attempting to tune up without success. This is a far cry from the joyous chorus of the toads that emerge after the summer rains. There have been many nights when I've lain awake and listened to their hallelujah chorus, a clamor for life and a mate to share all with.

Two mourning doves and a belted kingfisher sit on opposite ends of the electric wire, the kingfisher looking like a kid with a bad haircut, the doves graceful as all doves are, while out in the pasture the white-winged doves hoot and holler, and the mockingbird, perched at the top of a Goldwater pine, does his best to mimic everything. I have tried teaching him the happy little refrain from Hayden's "Surprise" Symphony, thus far without success.

On my way back to the house, I walk through the carport where every summer for the past four years swallows have nested on top of the light fixture. This means that for five months the car will be covered with everything that falls out of the nest; irritating to be sure, but it wouldn't be summer without the constant coming and going of those kite-like bodies, the constant twittering that accompanies the family, and the pure pleasure of seeing these birds in flight. The nest also necessitates caging our two orange porch cats on the days when the youngsters first take to the air.

Inside, where I come to write, I look out my study window thirty miles up the valley, most of which is the way it has been for centuries — framed by mountains, crisscrossed by washes that flow during the rainy season, painted here and there with the green of mesquite, the starry blossoms of desert willow.

Two feeders hang from the branches of the chinaberries that shade the windows, and the trees are alive with the chatter of small birds — white-crowned sparrows, finches, the splendid *Pyrrhuloxia,* breast streaked with fuschia, a hepatic tanager the color of a pomegranate flower, a flash of lemon yellow as the Scotts oriole comes looping in.

And beyond, where I scatter grain on the ground, the quail, both scaled and gambrel, both with their distinctive topknots, waddle and peck.

Ostensibly my study is for writing, but I have spent hours here watching, listening, marveling over the shapes and habits, the coloration and feathered design of even the most common sparrow.

Now from the reeds beside the pond comes the song of a red-winged blackbird, that cheerful fluting that blesses marshy places across America. I open the windows wide, hear the thrasher's wolf-whistle, a yel-low-throat singing *witchy-witchy*, the bull-frogs' bass continuo, and behind it all the perfect silence that is at the heart of earth, the white page upon which symphonies are written.

Mountain Time

Earth turns on its axis, spins through limitless space. In August it comes within range of the Perseid Meteors, a shower of débris that, entering our orbit, catches fire and burns across the night sky before turning to dust.

It was at Sunglow Ranch that I saw my first meteors. We set up chairs in the east pasture and waited, heads tilted back, naming the constellations that we knew, then sitting in silence, waiting. Around us were mountains, black on blacker sky, and a herd of Black Angus steers, nearly invisible and oblivious to us or to the fiery descent of what have wrongly been labeled "falling stars."

That night the sky blazed with uncountable streaks of silver, and, in accordance with superstition, I made wishes — all of them the same. That somehow I could stay in this desert country forever.

Twenty years later I sit on our stone patio on a night scented by approaching rain. Cottonwood leaves rustle. Crickets shrill, and in the pond the frogs bellow like sackbuts.

Glenn has gone to bed, leaving me with Mucho, our old black Lab, who is lying on my feet. In spite of a few clouds, the stars are visible — Big Dipper, Milky Way, North Star, Pleiades — and suddenly a display of meteors unlike any I have ever seen begins in the northeastern sky. Thousands of them burst into fire, zip across the darkness, an explosion almost audible.

Without warning, the air crackles with what sounds like static electricity, and, turning, I watch wings of flame streak down the valley — orange, blue, incandescent red, gone before I can grasp the actuality, burnt out, vanished in the dark.

There are always words that, like this reverse phoenix, hover beyond reach, thoughts that tantalize then vanish, leaving frustration, anguish at my own inability to capture them, and so it is on this night.

Many years ago, I said to the harpsichordist Alan Curtis that I was always searching for something for which there were no words or means of grasping them.

"Does this happen in music, too?" I asked, needing corroboration from a dear friend who was also a musician at the height of his career.

He looked at me out of eyes as blue as the sea and smiled, a poignant quirking of his lips. "All the time," he said sadly. "All the time." And I remember how his long, supple pianist's hands moved out, groped, as if in supplication to the gods.

At the time I was comforted. I was no longer alone, for here was a master who had experienced the same frustration. Those who struggle with music and literature are always banging heads against the wall of the untransmittable. The magical ability to communicate has always been and will remain in the realm of the Muse, who smiles or does not depending on circumstance.

Who can say where a poem — or an idea for a story — has its beginning? Not I. What I do know is that one morning I sat looking out the window at the Chiricahuas that were home and refuge to the Apaches, and to Geronimo, that fierce warrior whose face had haunted me for many years, and a voice that seemed to come out of the rock formed words — Geronimo's words — that I wrote down and never changed.

Since then I have read this poem to a hundred audiences, and it has never failed to raise the hair on my head — or to elicit a similar response in the listeners.

Why? I believe that somehow, in the magic that surrounds these mountains, echoes of those who lived here remain, that the mountains keep a time that is not ours and cannot be reckoned by clocks or calendars. In that time, voices can be heard if we take the time to listen.

This is difficult for we who live in a modern, computerized world. We are not accustomed to sitting still, without the intrusion of television or computer monitor, and listening to the earth. Pity us. For the land has lessons to teach, music to spill out on the wind.

And on the Second Day . . .

We are on our way home from the Rocky Mountain Book Fair in Denver, heading south on Interstate 25, when Glenn says: "You've never seen the aspens change."

When I tell him I've never even seen an aspen, he says: "Hang a right at the next exit." The West is mapped in his head; the geography of the land over which he flew for a quarter century is engraved in his memory.

Miles later, we are in the San Juan Mountains of Colorado — gray granite peaks sharp against October blue sky, steep slopes washed by rivers of gold. Not the gold sought by prospectors, but living color, gold in ceaseless motion, dancing, twisting, catching the light and throwing it back into the dazzling air.

Long ago, as a young child smitten by the beauty of the world, I discovered the ability of words to preserve it. As an adolescent wanting desperately to paint but lacking the talent, I made a second discovery — that I could let scenes paint themselves on the lenses of my eyes leaving a lasting imprint strengthened by language, a monologue that rises from within, a stream flowing upward against gravity, a gift I could not then and cannot now explain.

We stop by a grove of white-trunked aspens. Graceful, gilt-crowned, they form a natural cathedral, its dome a twining arch of leaves and supple branches that Brunelleschi would have envied.

Cathedrals are made for prayer, and prayer comes easily here, with the yellow light falling as though through stained glass, dappling the grassy floor, the leaves murmuring gently like monks at Vespers. I tilt up my face and am blessed by a fall of golden rain.

On the road once more, Glenn again consults his internal map and says: "You've never been to Monument Valley. Since we're this far. . . ." His words dwindle, and he looks at me out of the corner of his eye.

The highway stretches out, bends around a mountain, dips down to a nameless river, and I feel the tug and pull of adventure drawing me on, an excitement common to all travelers eager to see beyond the next curve, to climb mountains simply because they are there.

Who has first come upon Monument

Valley — its spires, mesas, hoodoos, spindles of red rock — in the midst of storm? As we take the narrow road out onto the desert floor, thunder rips the silence, lightning zigzags through dark sky. Around us the great monoliths are wreathed in cloud, rising out of mist as if just summoned from the impenetrable depths of earth.

We are witness, I think, to the second day of Creation. **And God said let the dry land appear; and it was so**. We are two small humans in a car, looking out, coming close to what I can only call an edge, a stepping over into antiquity, a time of upheaval and myth. The old gods of the Navajos are here, too, in the great rocks, in the slivers of lightning, in the drums that beat in the sky.

The next day we drive to Mexican Hat, a small village on the bluffs above the San Juan River that is running red with red earth and full to its banks.

On our return, the sun breaks through clouds, and mesas, monuments, the wind-shaped forms of the remains of mountains thrust up captured and held in an immensity of air.

I feel my heart cracking. There are places on earth too magnificent to take within. And then Glenn says: "I've been wanting to take you to the Grand Cañon. I want to see your face when you see it."

The Grand Cañon has always been, to me, a name to which I have given no pictorial foresight, perhaps wisely, knowing intuitively that there are places beyond imagining.

We wind our way though miles of desert cut by long mesas, through Tuba City, the name of which intrigued my friend Ed Ochester, director of the Pitt Poetry Series and himself a fine poet, to the point where he once said to me he'd always wanted to go there.

Now I can tell him that he does not — that Tuba City is like Gallup or any other poor town of the region, with enclaves of rusting trailers, tumbleweeds piled against miles of sagging fence, and the desert stretching away, its sand dotted with scrub grass and scrawny trees.

On and on. I am blinded by distance, stunned into incoherence. What must they have thought, those early pioneers used to the dense forests, the low, pale skies of the East? Did they feel as I do that the world goes on into infinity, blending with sky, luring with its clarity? Did some place within bleed with longing, ache with the inability to describe what surrounded them? I want to cover my eyes, put my head in my lap, and cry out: "No more! No more!"

But there is always more, and I must look. I may never pass this way again, or if I do, it will not be like the first time — an end to innocence.

We stand at the first look-out above a cleft in the rock so deep, so terrifying that the breath is sucked out of my lungs.

Nothing could have prepared me for this — not any photograph, not any word in any language known.

For the sake of sanity, I focus on the small — a ragged pine tree a thousand feet below. It juts out into space, and from one brush-stroke branch a raven casts off, glides on an invisible current of air, lower and lower into the cañon's red maw.

For a moment I become that bird, that minute black speck drifting in unconquered space, down and down through layers of rock and time, lost to everything but air.

Beside me Glenn says: "What do you say now?"

I clutch the rail with both hands, draw a deep breath, shake my head. "Nothing," I whisper. "Nothing at all."

I am back twenty years pounding on the wall that separates me from self and words. Quite simply, there are no words.

People from all nations cluster around us. Like me, they stand stunned and mute, made conscious of the fact that no work of man can rival this one act of nature; that no poem, symphony, painting, or photograph can capture or express this explosion of awful beauty.

I would like to stand here for the rest of my life, saying nothing, while the rain sweeps over me, and the wind; while the striations of rock change colors and the sun rises and falls behind mountains and the far-off curve of horizon, and a solitary raven etches with black wings on transparent canvas.

I would like to be turned into the stone under my feet, to give myself over, not in defeat but in triumphal communion with the mighty.

Horses, Horses, Horses

We came to the San Simon Valley with four horses — the old ones, Jefe and Dolf — and two young Thoroughbreds, black Doc and chestnut Dandy.

From the first day when I saw Doc in a corral at the Lazy V Seven, a training facility belonging to our neighbors, Wayne and Glenda Rottweiler, I was in love.

"What horse is that?" I asked.

"Oh, that's old Dirty," Glenda said.

Even from across the yard, the black hide shone like polished obsidian. "What kind of a name is that?" I asked, insulted on Dirty's behalf.

Glenda laughed. "He's registered as I Fight Dirty. Don't ask me how people name horses. We've been using him as a pony horse at the track, but he's for sale."

A neighbor, Guy Miller, once observed that love of horses is a congenital disease that is never cured and only gets worse, and I am living proof of that theory.

"Can I try him?" I asked Glenda.

All that was needed was interest. Within

minutes I was mounted on the huge black that had won his first race by twenty lengths and then decided he'd rather sniff the daisies and was retired.

Some horses are born with the determination to out-run all others. These are the champions of record. The rest end up in riding stables, or as jumpers, pony horses, or used for pleasure. There are, however, more horrible alternatives I can't bear to think about. Out here, one of those alternatives is stated simply as: "Going to the killers." I can never hear those words without shivering. Only the cold-blooded could sell a friend, a living, breathing animal by the pound.

I took Dirty onto the training track and walked him a short way, then asked for a lope, not before settling myself firmly in the saddle. But I could feel him questioning me through the reins, and through his big body. "A lope? Not a gallop?"

I answered. "Easy."

He obliged. It was like riding a floating leaf, smooth, graceful, responsive. In fact, it was hardly like riding at all, and I fell in love the way one does with Thoroughbreds and their great, beating, loyal hearts.

Several years later, at the Cowboy Hall of Fame to receive my first Western Heritage

Award, I was talking to Richard Farnsworth, one of my all-time favorite Western actors and a splendid horseman. He asked what horses we owned, and I told him about Dirty whom I'd renamed Doc in honor of Doc Holliday.

Richard's blue eyes lit up. "I just love Thoroughbreds," he said. "They give you all they have straight from their hearts."

Truly spoken. Unfortunately in Doc's case, all he had wasn't enough.

Once home, I discovered the first problem. Doc wouldn't stand tied, in fact went dangerously berserk if he found himself restrained by rope or rein. To be anywhere near his twelve hundred pounds when he panicked was asking for serious injury or death.

I worked around this at first, saddling him in his pen, attempting to get him used to the sight of a rope, even sending him off to a trainer who returned him after three months in the same frame of mind as when he'd left.

But there are always times when a horse has to be tied and is expected to stand still and behave, as when it's being shod or when the rider has to dismount on the trail for any reason. What I had was a horse I couldn't trust, no matter how much I wanted to.

Had I been able to ride or work with Doc

daily, it might have been possible to overcome his second problem, which was that he was tireless, as fresh after twenty miles as he'd been at the start. In fact, once I loaned him to a responsible rancher for use in a week-long roundup. He came back shaking his head. "You know," he said, "you can't wear that horse down. He's always got an edge on him, even after twelve hours' work."

Glenn, who was recovering from seven broken ribs and a broken collar bone, courtesy of Dandy who'd decided to buck when Glenn had one foot in the stirrup and bailed off onto a row of rocks, looked at me. "Get rid of him," he said. "That horse will kill you."

How could I sell Doc, the horse of my dreams, the creature I loved, and who, for a certainty, loved me? Who watched for me over the fence, nickered a welcome, shoved his head against me like a dog, and huffed deep in his chest when I touched him? The horse that I had trained to lower his head and open his mouth to take the bit, to stand still as a stone while I scrambled into the saddle?

I'd taught him to trot again, as, in his pony horse life, he'd somehow forgotten that natural gait, and I'd discovered he had another gait, a lovely, single-foot that was a joy to ride.

I'd nursed him through a serious accident when somehow he'd run a stick through his foreleg clear to the bone. For hours I sat in his stall talking, singing, urging him to recovery, and knowing through human-horse osmosis that, for me, because of me, he'd make it.

Love flowed between us in an almost visible stream. I was living *My Friend Flicka*, and how I wanted to believe in the happy ending!

As a child I believed in the happy endings of all the horse books I devoured at a sitting and then re-read until the books were worn. If one little boy could tame the Black Stallion, why could not I, a grown woman, do the same with a horse that had a simple hang-up?

But life does not always parallel art. The day came when Glenn and I were out for a ride, and Doc kept fussing with his bit, tossing his head as if bothered by the fit of the metal bar in his soft mouth.

Finally I dismounted to check, keeping the reins firmly in hand. For a reason I'll never know, Doc took fright, hauled back, and half reared, pulling the reins away. Then he bolted, headed for home at racehorse speed — thirty miles an hour. A natural jumper, he cleared the four-foot gate at the driveway and was still careening around the stable yard when Glenn and I arrived a while later — me on foot.

Somehow in his mad gallop, Doc had managed to step on the dragging reins and lose his bridle, and until he settled down there was no way I could catch him. I didn't try, just set about unsaddling Glenn's horse and ignoring my own, knowing that at the sight of the usual chores — and the sound of the grain bin opening — Doc's stomach and not love would triumph. As it did.

Soon he was standing at the hitching rail, blowing, sweating, foam-flecked but calm — another horse entirely. Looking at him, no one could have imagined the scene of minutes before.

I unsaddled him, brushed him down, hosed him off, and gave him a handful of oats — just one — not as a reward for good behavior, either. There is simply no point punishing a horse long after the cause. He had forgotten — if he'd ever known.

Glenn had not. "You could have been on him," he said, fear and concern plain on his face. "I want you to get rid of this horse."

I didn't answer. The truth was obvious. I could, indeed, have been on him, could have stayed on him, too, even over that four-foot gate. But a horse in a blind panic is a danger not only to the rider but to itself. One false step, one hole in the ground, and horse and rider fall in a tangle of thrashing legs and broken bodies. I've seen it happen. Once. That was enough.

I never rode Doc again. Cautiously, like a parent seeking a family for a beloved child, I put out the word that Doc was for sale. Several offers were refused because I could foresee he'd be ruined by the buyers — people to whom he was simply an animal to be used and discarded like a pair of worn-out shoes, to be misunderstood and beaten for one wrong move.

Finally I accepted the offer of the son of a neighbor, a real horseman who ran a sprawling dairy farm in New Mexico and who would — I hoped — use Doc wisely and well.

He was loaded into the trailer, and I stood watching, hands clenched, a lump like a rock in my throat. A last, lingering dream of childhood was being severed — that hope, faith, belief in the magic of love between human and horse — and the fact that Doc thrust his magnificent head over the side and neighed loudly, poignantly all the way down the lane did nothing to help. We both knew that something irreplaceable had been lost.

That night, and every night for three months, I wept in the bathtub, wept in secret, for I knew Glenn would buy him back if I told him how I felt. In fact, a year later when I did mention it, he said: "If I'd known it was that bad, I'd have bought him back. Hell, we could've kept him just to look at!"

I shook my head. Once was more than enough.

From my study window I can see Jefe running the fence line in the north pasture. He is showing off for the red mare and the gray Arab filly in the pasture across the lane.

Glenn comes in and watches the performance over my shoulder. "It's a real pleasure to know him, isn't it?" he says as he has said many times before.

"I may be growing older, but I refuse to grow up," I answer, quoting the bumper sticker.

At thirty, Jefe still moves as if he's on springs and has developed a fan club of admirers from the vet to friends, all of whom are impressed with his vitality and spirit.

He reaches the corner, slides to a stop, bucks, and begins galloping back. The "girls" hang their heads over the fence, obviously fascinated, and I remember the day at Rancho Milagro when the hired man from the Lazy V Seven telephoned in a state of panic.

"Your stallion's down here running the mares," he said. "I can't get near him."

Stallion? Of course, I knew it was Jefe, accompanied by Dolf, and both of them in big trouble. In human parlance, Jefe is "proud," which means that when he was gelded the job wasn't complete, so he has just enough testosterone surging through him to give the desire, the high-spirited drive of a stallion.

At one time, and possibly still, this was a common practice in Mexico where the adjective *macho* can be applied to both horse and rider, and where a horse with the spirited temperament of a stud is much admired. It is a practice that dates back to the days of the Spanish conquest, when no self-respecting Spaniard would be seen riding a mare.

Glenn was at Rancho Milagro that day, and we threw saddles, halters, lead ropes, and bridles into the bed of the truck and took off, cursing. Horses! With horses, it's always some crisis!

On our way down the road, we spotted

the opening in the fence where the two bad boys saw their chance to go exploring and, naturally, took it. Horses have radar. Leave a gate open or a fence down anywhere within a mile, and they will know and go through within five minutes.

We pulled into the stable yard and went out to the pasture that was alive with running, spotted bodies — a scene from the annals of the Nez Percé, those long-ago breeders of fine Appaloosas.

Jefe was rounding up his mares, circling them at top speed, his tail a black flag, his neck outstretched, his teeth bared, ready to nip the disobedient into submission. Dolf, ever the faithful Leporello, had backed Jerry, the old nurse gelding, into a corner and was keeping him there. The gentlest of horses around people, Dolf served no animal master but Jefe, a trait that caused us problems as when he attempted to savage an equine newcomer.

We stood watching for a minute, and Jefe's intent became clear. He was going to bring the herd of mares to his own domain like any mustang stallion. *Droit de seigneur* was in his heart, his blood, his every move, deluded though he was.

Without discussion or thought I did something that, looking back, causes me to wonder at my own foolishness. I picked up a halter and lead rope and without hesitation stepped into the mêlée.

Bodies swerved past me. I was surrounded by the pounding hoofs of frightened and wild-eyed mares, but I kept on walking.

"Jefe!" I called as he thundered past. "Easy! Whoa, old man!"

He slid to a stop, nostrils wide, and looked at me. He was ready to bolt, but, unlike Doc, he was thinking. Unlike Doc, *he obeyed.* That made all the difference.

I kept on talking, a stream of sound. At times like this, it's the calming voice that matters more than the words. He pricked up his ears, listened, and stayed put. Reaching him, I slipped on the halter, fastened it, picked up the lead rope, and began walking away. Reluctantly he followed, turning back once or twice to neigh at what would have been his captives.

Without their leader, the mares began to wander off. Some grazed, others still watched Jefe, half inclined to come along. Dolf, understanding that the caper had ended, released Jerry with a nip on his rump and ambled toward Glenn, eyes shining. I could almost hear him saying: "We had a real adventure!"

Beside me, Jefe was slick with sweat. He danced and tossed his head, still thinking that I might relent, that he might get away. When I put a hand on his shoulder, I felt him trembling, his muscles taut. He'd given in, but the instinct that drove him was strong, and will always be there just beneath the skin, making demands he does not, cannot understand.

Together we walked home across the mile of pasture. The grasses bent in a steady south wind; the sun was touching the top of the Huachuca Mountains. Nearly feeding time. By the time I turned him loose in his pen, he'd cooled off and was nudging me with his nose as if the incident had never happened.

After many years, I know that he and I are as close as horse and master can be. Between us flows all the love, trust, and response that was lacking between Doc and me. Spirited, possibly abused, and almost surely misunderstood by some past owner, nevertheless Jefe gives when I ask and I respect him for that and for what he is — a delightful companion. A real pleasure to know.

The old road to Globe out of Pomerene follows the San Pedro River and seems not to have changed since the days when Pearl Hart and Joe Boot made their getaway from the stage hold-up at Cane Springs.

Ancient mesquites crowd the narrow shoulder for miles, and behind them, barely visible, slabs of gray rock rise like sleeping mammoths, scoured, cracked by wind and weather.

On this spring morning, the river is only a trickle of brown water, and the temperature climbs with the sun. Inevitably I put myself in place of the early settlers — those who attempted to ranch or farm without benefit of air conditioning, supermarkets, and shelter save that which they built with their own labor.

How long ago it seems, and yet how close, particularly in these isolated places out of sight of towns or civilization. I open the window. The scent of water comes in, and with it the sweetness of blooming palo verde trees, along with several flies.

There were flies in the old days, too, and biting midges and mosquitoes along the river — and the malaria that no one remembers any more. They were a tough breed, those old-timers, those outlaws and rustlers who rode this trail and lived to tell about it — or to keep their secrets.

We're headed to Globe in hope of finding

some record of Big Nose Kate's sojourn there. As she put it in her memoir, she "opened a hotel." Whether true or false, no one seems to know, and in Globe I have no success finding any records. The town has been destroyed several times — by Pinal Creek in raging flood, and by fire — and its records, its secrets are gone as well. What remains are stories, some real, some imagined, all worth listening to.

What I do find is first-hand knowledge of Pearl Hart, Arizona's "Bandit Queen," who stuck up the stage in May, 1899, ran for her life, was captured, tried, and sentenced to five years in the infamous Yuma Prison. Released early — possibly because she was pregnant — she went briefly on the musical circuit, then married and settled down to a life of ease — and silence. Whoever, whatever she was, she never spoke of it, and took what she, alone, knew to the grave with her in 1956.

My head is buzzing with what I know will be my next novel, following *Doc Holliday's Woman*. Everything seems to click into place, bringing with it a rush of adrenaline. Research is exciting, intriguing, part of the fun of writing. It's like setting out to do an enormous puzzle with half the pieces missing or lost.

And then — I find a horse.

On the desk in the motel is a chamber of commerce directory listing local attractions, among which is a Paso Fino horse farm. As always, I'm curious.

"Let's go look," I say to Glenn. "I've never seen a Paso Fino."

"Why not?"

Carol de Nino meets us at her gate. Behind her are barns and a corral full of horses — small, muscular creatures with eye-catching heads. Neither Thoroughbreds nor Arabians, nor anything in between, these are horses out of antiquity, living statues.

Carol explains. "An old breed . . . similar to the Spanish Barb. They say Columbus brought the first ones on his second voyage to America. And don't be confused by the name. These are *not* Peruvian Pasos. These are Paso Finos, named for one of their gaits. They do a four-beat lateral gait instead of a trot, and it's a smooth ride. Would you like to try one?"

Did she have to ask?

She comes back leading a sturdy, blood bay gelding with the finest eyes I've ever seen. Large, wide-set, a golden amber, they observe the world with calm dignity, capture my reflection so I see myself, hand outstretched in honorable greeting.

"What's your name?" I whisper to the questing nostrils, the ear turned toward me.

"Canelo el Grande," Carol answers.

"What's that mean?"

She laughs. "Nothing. There is no such word as Canelo, but whoever named him didn't know it."

When he's been brushed and saddled, Carol puts him through his paces — Paso Fino, Paso Corto, Paso Largo — three versions of his four-beat gait, then she dismounts and hands me the reins. "All yours. I'll saddle up, and we'll go out."

Canelo is fourteen and one half hands, his back eight inches lower than Doc's. There's no need for me to search for a handy rock or hay bale with this horse. I'm in the saddle in one motion, and he stands still, waiting his cue.

It's astonishing! The Paso Fino gait is not like riding at all. It's not a pace, is, in fact, almost the same as Doc's single-foot, but smoother, the steps shorter and more rhythmic. *Ta dum, ta dum, ta dum, ta dum.* I can hear each hoof hit the ground while feeling no jolt.

What this means is no more posting to a rough trot, or sitting and taking it while my teeth rattle. Can he lope? I ask for one and get the easiest lope I ever sat.

Am I falling in love again? Not yet. One learns caution in matters of the heart, or should.

Carol comes out riding a young filly and takes the lead. We go up a hill, then through what appears to be a dumpsite filled with rusted machinery, twisted pieces of metal and old wire, each and every thing enough to spook a nervous horse. Canelo winds his way through, unconcerned, then moves into the slowest of his gaits as we cross a wash.

"How long can he keep this up?" I ask.

"All day if he's in shape."

Jefe is getting old, and I, much as it's a hard fact to swallow, am heading into middle age. I've had my love affair. It's time to settle down with a seasoned, intelligent animal, one not predisposed to throw ignorant fits and kill me.

As if reading my mind, Carol says: "He's for sale."

Having learned that it's "buyer beware," when horse-trading, I ask: "Why?" Not that I expect an honest answer.

"Because I bought him for a customer who didn't like his color. And now I'm stuck."

A look at her face says she's telling the truth. My own face must express absolute astonishment. That someone would turn down a splendid animal, one with perfect color even down to the black dorsal stripes and the line in the center of his back, is the most nonsensical reason I have ever heard.

And so the little misnamed and unwanted blood bay became mine within minutes and was renamed six months later after we learned about each other and, yes, learned to love. It's not a glamorous name, not one befitting his nobility or the line of glamorous ancestors, but it fits. Peanut we named him, and Peanut he is, every tough, dauntless, red-skinned inch.

From a Chinese Vase

The Great Blue Heron stands motionless above his own reflection. Which is more real, bird or image?

Water gives life to the bird mirrored on its slightly rippling surface, captures the metallic blue-gray body, the small head poised, alert for any sign of frog or dragonfly.

The frogs have hidden deep in weeds and mud, but eventually one will show itself, and the heron, in a move too swift to record, will have his meal. Then he'll retreat, walking slowly on hinged legs, to the bank under the cottonwood where he will digest in shady comfort.

Herons have fascinated me since I first saw them in the Pymatuning Swamp in northwestern Pennsylvania. Then, as now, they seemed birds from a Chinese vase, the sinuous curves of their great bodies mimicking the shape of a man-made urn, although in flight they resemble pterodactyls more than the sensual renderings of the Orient.

Certainly I never expected to find herons

in the desert. These are birds of marsh and open water, their diet of fish and frogs not in great supply in the Southwest. Yet here they are, male and female, for I have seen them together, and last year I found a young one in the weeds at the edge of the lane — unafraid but obviously searching for its meal in the wrong place.

Our heron, too, is quite tame. Often I have watched him standing among the horses who come to splash in the pond and who ignore him as if he is a tree or fence post, nor does our presence frighten him. Perhaps he realizes that we are fascinated by his beauty, curious about his habits, or perhaps hunger drives him to indifference. Who can say?

What I know is that I have sat close to him for hours, while the bright orange dragonflies hover and dart over the water, and the blue damsel flies weave through the grasses, while the vermilion flycatcher swoops down from a branch, an explosion of flame, and around us the world hums with the voices of living things.

It was April in Willa Cather country — the Nebraska plains and sandhills, the great Platte River that braids itself around islands and banks in time with its own flowing.

I had been asked to participate in the Plains Writers Series, and so made my first visit to the poignant and changeable landscape that Cather captured so well.

At Kearney, billboards welcomed **Crane Watchers**, and my response was instantaneous. All my life I had been curious about sandhill cranes, had read descriptions, heard them talked about, but the need to see them for myself was vital.

We were staying with Don Welch, an extraordinary poet and professor at Kearney, and his wife, Aline, and, when I asked him about the cranes, his eyes brightened.

"Come on," he said, already reaching for his jacket. "We'll go out to the river. They'll be coming back for the night pretty soon."

And there, in a stubble field by the Platte, I was surrounded by beating wings, the haunting cry that, once heard, can never be forgotten — an ancient music that stirs a primal response in the listener, a wildness not completely vanquished by the meaningless noises of civilization.

I filled my eyes with the magnificent grace of feathered bodies — their swift descent and preliminary dance of courtship. It was a damp, gray late afternoon, with the scent of rain — or snow — heavy in the air, but in memory I am standing in a bubble of light, a chamber that echoes and reëchoes down all the years of my life.

It is Christmas, 1997. I have taken my mother to Mass in the little church of San Felipe Neri in Rodeo.

The town is quiet. Somewhere a dog barks; a coyote yips in answer. Somewhere a piñon fire is burning, and the fragrance, so typical of Southwest winters, makes me stop and raise my head, sniff the sweetness that is like cloves and cinnamon and the heart of the wood.

It has been cloudy all day, with periods of sleet and wet snow. The sky above the Chiricahuas is dark, and the peaks are blurred in mist. Suddenly the clouds part, letting a yellow beam of sun fall through, and in the distance, too far away to identify, the singing begins, rooting me in place. What? I ask silently. What?

Then I see them, high overhead in the gap in the clouds — a long, tattered ribbon of flying cranes, each with a voice that answers another, voices of wilderness and lonely places, chords not written by any human, but which strike deeply, resonating in my bones.

Too quickly they are out of sight, but I can hear them long after they vanish behind the mountains, and I think I have received the finest Christmas blessing of all — a gift of music, poetry, and the holiness of all life.

Stone Houses

The people of the stone houses are gone,
whirled like chaff over dry fields,
scattered by the war dances of dust devils.

What remains —
sculpted walls, curved shards,
small stores of corn —
says little.

What we know is that they lived like birds.
That from their doorways
they looked out and out
over shimmering trees
into the arms of sky,

and that one day, light-boned,
weightless as any winged flock
before a journey,
they rose and flew.

From *No Roof But Sky*

Petroglyphs

From this high up, I see what eagles see, and hawks. From here the San Simon Valley spreads out like a river, running north and south. Beyond the Peloncillos, the Animas Range challenges sky with sharp teeth.

At my back, a sheer cliff rises several hundred feet. I'm on a ledge on the eastern face of the Chiricahuas where, perhaps a thousand years ago, there was a home in a cave in the core of the mountain.

Whoever lived here has left a record carved in the rock — a handprint, a spiraling circle, a figure trapped in rhyolite. I think it was a woman who, like me, stood looking out, eyes narrowed against the glare. I think she opened her arms and encompassed the valley, calling it hers, and then chiseled what she knew into stone — a message, an impulse to capture time, leave a mark that spoke of her existence.

On the edge of the cliff is a shoulder-high boulder, its top hollowed like a bowl from water that drips steadily down from an unseen source as it has for centuries.

Whoever lived here had running water at their door — and security. No one can approach this place unseen. And summer and winter the cave, its walls smoke-blackened from long dead fires, maintains a steady temperature.

The rising sun touched the woman awake, passed overhead, and disappeared so that the mountain cast its purple shadow long before night when she was the first to see the moon rise and pour its light across familiar terrain.

I stand lost in the spiral of the petroglyphs, the circling of time. Everything is as it was and will be — mountain, valley, water, sky.

Tsankawe Mesa

The trail to the top of Tsankawe Mesa is worn six inches deep into the soft, volcanic rock. I walk carefully, fitting my feet into the narrow space — one, then another directly in front. Near the top, the path squeezes through a gap between high walls, barely wide enough for a person. The Old Ones were smaller than I and, I think, tireless, for although the climb isn't steep, it's steady and tricky.

The view from the top of the mesa is endless, three hundred and sixty degrees. Northern New Mexico, its mountains, forests, tiers of similar mesas surround me in this little known, unexplored place of antiquity.

Nothing stops the wind here. It blows steadily, bending the rough grasses, the orange globe mallows and yellow crown beards, fluttering the white petals of prickly poppies and humming, always humming, in my ears.

I walk carefully past mounds of dirt, step around what must have been a primitive *kiva* dug in the center of clustered dwellings built of mud that has melted down, returned to earth leaving only traces of those who lived here, whose feet wore a trench in rock.

Around me, pottery shards, black on white, nestle among small stones. Everywhere are remnants of a people who vanished, as all of the cliff and mesa dwellers vanished, into mystery and time. It is the fact of the shards that brings them to life. Here were humans who valued beauty as well as necessity, who fashioned bowls, jugs, storage jars to give pleasure while serving a definite function.

I know that the women laughed and gossiped as they shaped the clay, painted it using primitive brushes and pigment from the hearts of plants, while, around them, children tumbled in the grass, waved make-believe spears and stone axes, tossed crude balls, and laughed their own delight at being in such a place. I know that then, as now, the wind was humming, and beyond it the silence, deep as a well.

My reverie is shattered by the sound of voices. Four people emerge from below, tourists, speaking German, gazing around not at the view but at the ground.

One of them, an older woman, unfolds two brown shopping bags and begins to fill them, scooping up shards without consideration or conscience.

Of course, she must know that nothing is to be disturbed or taken from here. There are warning signs everywhere in several languages. Of course, she knows, but pretends ignorance, and I feel violated, as if it is my home whose ashes she is raking through.

I struggle to find the words to tell her. *"Verboten,"* I say after a minute, pointing to the half-filled bags and shaking my finger. *"Verboten."*

She snorts, gives me a look out of sharp gray eyes behind spectacles that glint in the sun, then turns and walks away, clutching her booty.

There have always been those who plunder, who take what belongs to the world and hide it, perhaps because they have an emptiness that cannot be filled, a lack that feeds on the possession of objects.

I wonder what she will do with her stolen treasures? Will she keep them to herself? Display them in a glass cabinet for friends? Play with them like pieces of a puzzle that do not, will never, fit?

I sit down on the cliff edge, watch a thundercloud building far to the north, its purple shadow spreading across mesas and red rock cañons.

The tourists have gone. Once again I am alone with the silence, cherishing the perfection of a black on white shard that lies next to me. I pick it up and find that it fits as if it were fashioned for the palm of my hand.

Mesa Verde

Richard Wetherill, rancher and indefatigable explorer of ruins, discovered one of the largest of the cliff dwellings at Mesa Verde in 1888. He and his brother-in-law, Charlie Mason, were searching for cattle on the mesa top when it began to snow.

Riding perilously close to the edge of Cliff Cañon, they saw, through falling snow and bare tree branches, an enormous dwelling tucked into a cave under the lip of the mesa.

Together they climbed down and up

again, and found what Wetherill named Cliff Palace, a ruin that was as it had been left perhaps for over a thousand years.

Over and over I have imagined that day — the darkness of storm, the heavy snow falling, falling, painting the bare trees white, and the peculiar hush that snow gives to the air, each flake dampening sound. And the two men, dazed, disbelieving as the dwelling appeared — a mirage, a ghostly image in the fading light.

But neither imagination nor the printed word can give any idea of the enormity of the mesa itself. At least twenty miles long, it rises up out of the Colorado plain like a forested green island surrounded by a moat of grass, and the road to the top seems endless — climbing, curving, always avoiding the many cañons and their treasures.

Although I had visited other cliff dwellings in Arizona and New Mexico, and had written a poem about Mesa Verde, it had always seemed unreal, out of reach, a chimera that tantalized behind a veil of snow.

Now it was summer, and Glenn, my son Dan, and I were on our way home from Wyoming, making, as always, a detour to visit the city in the rock.

We parked and got out of the car, and, impatient, I ran to the cañon's edge. And there it was, like a magic lantern slide or a doll's house built of stone, appearing and disappearing behind the branches of trees in full foliage and tossing in the wind — a city in microcosm — walls, tower, crenellations, white stone against the dark depths of the cave.

In what has become a family joke, and in direct contrast with my response to the Grand Cañon, I proceeded to disgrace myself by uttering the first words that came out of my mouth.

I pointed, capered like a madwoman, and shouted: "Oh, shit! There it is!"

"Mom," Dan muttered. "Shut up." Then he moved as far away from me as possible, not wishing to be associated with the woman in jeans, boots, black and white checked shirt who was uttering profanities in a sacred place.

From behind me came Glenn's laughter, and I joined in. Would the Anasazi, the Old Ones who had lived here, have cared? Certainly not. In their houses, they laughed and swore and cried, and I am sure that, when they left, they wept for the loss, not only of their homes but for this place of austere beauty that had touched them, every one, in every moment of the day.

Why they left, where they went, remains a

mystery. Perhaps drought drove them away, or tribal warfare. Or plague, similar to the bubonic plague that even today appears in isolated cases in the Southwest.

All we do know is that an entire civilization was here one day and gone the next, leaving behind questions without answers and castles fashioned of durable stone.

Metates

We are riding a trail at the base of the mountain, and come upon the rock without warning, a flat-topped boulder as big as our living room, its surface hollowed at regular intervals, a community *metate,* where once six or eight women knelt and ground corn and acorns, their brown arms laboring, moving back and forth, back and forth, keeping rhythm like a pulse.

The boulder, high on a rise, has a view up and down the valley. Were these Apache women who sat here beside a wash that must have, then, run year 'round — or their ancestors, perhaps the woman of the cliff, a cave dweller older than time — who discovered the art of making flour from native plants, who survived, year after year doing what was necessary?

Always we come back to the simplicity of

"making do," of living off the earth and one's own labor. Always, we come back to basics — food, shelter, survival. Will we, in my lifetime or the next, come back to this again?

Will there come a time in the future when someone comes across the ruins of this house of ours, this garden we have planted and nurtured, the descendants of our beans, corn, peppers, squash, rose bushes, the rock walls, and wonder as I wonder now — *who was it who lived here? Who was it that left their mark?*

Splangish

Jesús came to us shortly after we moved here, a small, dark man of many talents except that of speaking English. Thanks to him, we have fenced pastures, rock walls, a stone patio, and a woodshed stacked with mesquite logs, in addition to an ever-growing fund of humorous stories. Take today.

It is 6:45 A.M. I am in robe and slippers recovering from a ten-day bout with flu when Jesús bangs on the door. He communicates that Dolf is at the far end of the pasture in "*chan-cé* bad trouble."

By means of pantomime — Jesús clutching his crotch and repeating, "*muy grande,*" — I assume that Dolf is somehow having trouble with his private parts. So I take off, carrying a halter, slippers flopping in sand, stone, burrs, terrified at what I will find.

Breathless, I find Dolf and Jefe grazing peacefully, and no sign of elephantiasis of Dolf's . . . well, you know. I bend down and peer under his belly. *Nada.* I feel around

like Crocodile Dundee groping the trans-
vestite. Dolf bends his head around and
gives me a look I understand. It says: "What
in hell are you doing back there?"

"Nada," I say to him. "Forget it," and go
home followed by two horses that are
thinking carrots or apples, not gigantic erec-
tions.

Jesús is waiting on the porch. "OK?" he
asks.

"Nada," I answer, using one of my bona
fide fifty Spanish words.

He clutches his crotch again. "Me
watchee," he says. *"Muy grande."*

I shake my head. *"Es nada,"* I repeat, and
go in the house wondering if once again I've
misunderstood the whole scene and de-
ciding I haven't. Something must have been
wrong. It's my fault I didn't get it.

For Jesús to come to me, holding his
crotch, is unheard of. Any conversational or
pictorial sexual innuendo, at all, is unheard
of. I am not even permitted to use the word
huevo for egg in his presence — a word that
can mean, also, a testicle. He has scolded
me for this. I must not refer to male parts
even when speaking about eggs. I must call
them *blanquillos* — white things — or be
branded as a tough-talking female for whom
no decent male has any respect. I don't

know whatever happened to the standard *huevos rancheros* breakfast. It's not a subject I'm equipped to argue about.

All this is difficult. I speak Italian, some of which is easily understood, some of which I have replaced with "Border Spanish," and a lot of hand waving. As a result, I don't speak any recognizable language any more, which is irritating in the extreme. Sometimes even I don't know what I'm talking about.

Take for example the weekly shopping list which Jesús hands to me written in a mixture of Spanish, English, and some kind of phonics. **Cuely** heads the list. Now there's a stopper. I don't even know how to pronounce it, let alone identify it. So I point. He pantomimes drinking. Not *coca*, which he loves, but something else. I throw out suggestions. *Nada*. Then I get it. Kool Aid! We're both delighted with ourselves.

"Is this all?" I ask.

He shakes his head. No. There's something else.

"What?"

He waves his hands. "In *inglés*, me don' know."

"In *español?*"

He waves his hands harder in the universal gesture of frustration. "Me don' know in *español*, either."

But I do, suddenly, out of familiarity with the list. "Bologna!" I shout.

He grins. "*Sí, sí.* Bologna!" Again we congratulate ourselves on having cracked the language barrier.

Back home I deliver the groceries, and Jesús asks another riddle. "How you say *puerco con espinos* in *inglés?*"

What I see in my mind is a hog stuck with medieval lances. My imagination often gets me into trouble. "*¿Es muy grande?*"

"*Chico.*" He makes a shape the size of a small poodle with his hands.

A piglet. A squirrel. A woodchuck. Dear God, how do I say that in Spanish?

He squats, draws a picture in the sand, one picture being worth a thousand misunderstood words and gestures.

"A porcupine!" What could be simpler? A pig with spines. How dumb can I be?

This will be proved shortly.

One more question before the day ends. "You wan' me catchee *lumbre por el fuego?*" he asks.

Do I want firewood? Well, since it's about ninety degrees, I really don't need it. "*Mañana,*" I answer, pleased at having deciphered more code.

But Jesús is disappointed. His shoulders droop. I've done it again. What he meant was that he wanted to try out the fireplace he just finished building, never mind the temperature or the fact that on any other day, to "catchee *lumbre*," would mean, "to gather wood."

We have built what is called here "an Arizona room," basically a sun porch with south-facing windows, a stone-flagged floor, and, at the far end, a huge stone fireplace. My idea for crisp fall nights.

When asked if he knew about fireplace construction, Jesús nodded. "*Sí, sí*. Me know."

It certainly seemed so as he asked us to order chimney flues, *"rocas por fuego,"* — fire bricks — and various other necessities; as he measured and muttered and went out into the cañon to collect the proper size *rocas*, the right kind of *arena* — sand — to make his mortar.

Now finished, the fireplace is magnificent, worthy of a photo in *Architectural Digest*, so I give in and tell him to bring some *lumbre*, then watch as he lays a careful fire.

The chimney draws with a *whoosh* like a powerful vacuum cleaner, and we smile at each other. Then Jesús drops his bombshell with a few words and gestures. He has never before built a fireplace, has only watched the *viejos*, the old ones in Mexico, do it, and is, I would guess, mightily relieved that his structure performs as intended. It goes without saying that I, too, am relieved.

I swear I'm going to bear down and study Spanish, take an immersion course, listen to the stack of tapes I keep buying and hope to learn by osmosis — a vain wish. Learning a new language is plain hard work. It's memorization, repetition, intellectual labor, and there's no easy way around it. *Es mucho trabajo,* but me dooee. *Mañana.*

The Spanish Bit

One of Archie's treasures, that he was positive dated back to Coronado, was a heavy silver and iron spade bit he'd found when he was a boy.

He'd bring it out from the trunk he kept in a corner and, holding it in his gnarled hands, would tell the story — how he'd been riding through the San Pedro Valley and seen a glint of metal in the sand. How, curious, he dismounted and found, to his astonishment, the skeleton of a horse and the Spanish bit.

"I knew right off what it was," he'd say. "Those Spanish soldiers come this way looking for gold. Got as far as Kansas, so they say, and then come back empty-handed."

Of course, I knew that skeleton and bit could not have been there undiscovered and intact for over four hundred years, but I never said anything. Why destroy a dream? Why paint over the picture he saw so clearly, when it is a picture I myself have seen — an army of armored riders advancing down the broad valley between the Huachuca and Mule Mountains, following the course of the San Pedro River that rises in Mexico and flows north to join the Gila?

Today, the Coronado Monument sits high in the Huachucas. From that vantage point, it is possible to see a hundred miles or more into Mexico — to the dark mountain that is Cananea, to the forested San José Mountains, the empty valley between, grass-covered and shimmering in the heat. Cottonwoods grow along washes and the banks of the river, their green startling and welcome.

Look hard and they will be there, a mirage of soldiers, horses, priests bearing wooden crosses, Indians, and herds of cattle and sheep, all surging through heat and dust under banners proclaiming the might and glory of Spain.

On their way down the valley, Coronado found the same Indians — Pimas and Sobaipuris — that Father Eusebio Kino would find when he followed the same route some one hundred and fifty years later. Kino went as far as the Gila River before turning west. Coronado marched through the Galiuros into what is now New Mexico, and farther — to the plains of Kansas.

In a car, on modern highways, I have

made the same journey in several days. By horse and on foot, it would have been a nightmare — and was. For, although the army advanced ostensibly in peace, in the name of God and the crown of Spain, it wreaked havoc in many of the Indian villages and pueblos, plundering, burning, making irrational demands, and finally war on the native peoples — in one case burning one hundred of them at the stake.

In all respects the exploration was a disaster. The soldiers who had not been killed by native arrows and spears, or died of exposure during a particularly harsh winter, returned to Mexico without the gold they had expected to find, and with Coronado himself dazed from being kicked in the head by a running horse.

So, although I can scan the width of the valley, dream along with Archie and call up images of splendor and the whole colorful, clamorous pageant, disillusionment rides alongside, a grinning skeleton.

What happened to Archie's horse and rider, or who he was, we'll never know. He was, I'd guess, a Mexican riding with the preferred spade bit, one chased in silver, indicating he was a man of means or perhaps an outlaw running for his life. But the desert keeps its secrets well.

Buck

There must be a thousand cowboys named Buck scattered across the West, but our Buck was a true original — insouciant, illiterate, a top hand but so full of himself that being around him was sometimes a chore.

Buck said what he thought without regard for political correctness or any kind of social nicety. He called a spade a spade and be damned to the consequences, which accounted for the fact that, in his mid-twenties, he'd been fired from more jobs than most people have in a lifetime. He'd driven semis, strung fence, built and painted houses and barns, tended bar, cowboyed in six states, and been married twice. When he showed up in Palominas, it was with the woman he intended to marry but hadn't gotten around to yet. I enjoyed him thoroughly, even when he was driving me crazy.

He and Starla, his half-breed, soon-to-be bride, had rented the trailer where Floyd and Ruby had been living before Ruby's suicide. It was just across the yard from our own house, bordering the lane.

They arrived in a battered Ford pickup, in the bed of which were two Heeler dogs, a basket of kittens, saddles, blankets, and boxes of the accumulated junk of a roving cowboy — baling wire, rawhide ropes, bits and old leather cinches, water jugs and empty gasoline cans — anything that might, someday, come in handy, even a battered anvil.

Both Buck and Starla looked travel-worn when Glenn and I went out to meet them, and I decided to be neighborly. "Come to dinner," I said.

Buck's face lit up. "I'm so hungry my belly thinks my throat's cut."

Starla glared at him out of wicked black eyes. "Shut up," she hissed. "What kind of way is that to talk?"

"It's the truth, honey." Buck flashed his white teeth.

"Can I help you?" Starla looked at me with what passed for an apology.

"Not tonight. Come over when you're ready."

They came that night and every night for the next three months until we moved to the San Simon Valley. It seems there was no gas hookup in the trailer and no way to cook — or to bathe.

How had Ruby and Floyd managed? I wondered with a pang. And why hadn't they told us? We would have paid, and gladly, to see them taken care of — unlike our landlady who was off at the racetrack playing the horses and watching her own horses run — and, so I was told, dodging the taxman with some success.

Had Ruby and Floyd been afraid of us — or were they simply too beaten down, too accustomed to doing without? As always when I think about Ruby, it's with regret. Her life had to have been one of utter desperation of which I, to my shame, was unaware.

With Buck around, however, despair took a holiday. Buck bounced. Buck laughed. Buck teased, and Buck told stories with the in-born ability of a natural humorist and lover of life.

I wish I'd written down his tall tales. They'd have made a book. As it was, some of his colorful and appropriate similes have become part of my own vocabulary.

At the ranch where he'd been hired, he was asked to break a particularly stubborn paint horse. Buck was a fine horseman, but he had his equine likes and dislikes, and he came into dinner one night grousing.

"Whoever bought that critter don't know

his face from a horse's ass. That horse has got a head like a pop cooler with nothin' inside, and he's mean as two buckets of snake shit besides. Pass them spuds, honey."

"Say please," Starla said.

"Aw, honey, come on. Quit tryin' to teach me manners. They just make things complexicated."

Starla set her jaw. She could look pretty mean herself without half trying, but Buck was undaunted, and simply reached across the table and grabbed the bowl of mashed potatoes. Starla pinched him. Hard.

Buck grinned. "Now be nice, honey," was all he said.

In addition to the horse with the pop-cooler head, Buck hated Jefe.

"I need to move a bull into the other pasture," he said one afternoon. "Glenn, why don't you come along?" He looked at me. "You can come, too, but keep a rein on that worthless horse of yours."

"He's not worthless!" If Buck and I disagreed on anything, it was Jefe.

"All he knows is to run, but come on anyhow and try to stay out of trouble."

Earlier Buck had driven a truck and trailer to the bull pasture. Our job was to get the bull into the trailer, which I knew wasn't going to be easy, given the normal attitude of bulls.

"He's over there in the brush," Buck said. "I'll go run him out. Don't let him get past you or we'll spend all day chasin' him."

Glenn looked at me. "You stay out of his way," he said. "You don't have to prove anything."

The bull charged out of the brush, with a kink in his tail. Seeing us, he whirled and went off in another direction with Buck and Glenn after him. Under me, Jefe gathered himself. Running was the game he knew best, bull or no bull. I held him in, then swung around to block the bull as he came back, tail up and blowing snot, the two men close behind.

The three of us surrounded him. All he had to do was go straight ahead into the trailer. Being what he was, he thought otherwise. Lowering his massive, horned head, he came for me, perhaps knowing I was the weak link. Jefe spun on his hind legs and bolted with the speed of a Quarter Horse ancestor, going flat out in several seconds and leaving the bull to eat his dust.

By the time I pulled up and rode back, Buck had his horse in the front of the trailer and a rope on the bull. He himself was on

232

foot, whacking the critter on the rump with the flat side of a shovel and cussing a blue streak.

It's been my observation that most animals understand cuss words. Mule skinners knew this, and so do I, having more than once cussed Jefe into obedience. But for whatever reason, the bull slowly and majestically complied and climbed into the trailer. Buck slammed the door on him and went around and reached over the side, freeing the rope from his saddle horn.

"I'm kind of glad Jefe can run," I remarked slyly.

Buck grunted. "Next time you go to buy a horse, get a good one and not some lump-jawed, hard-headed appy."

Some prejudices can never be overcome.

If only Buck had kept his opinions to himself. But if he had, he'd not have been who and what he was — a fine cowboy, quick to do what was needed with anything that came to hand. Like the time he and I came across a cow with a prolapsed uterus.

Buck had her roped, thrown, and tied before I knew what was happening. "Gimme that empty coke bottle in your saddlebag," he called over his shoulder.

"What for?"

"Geez! Just get over here and quit askin' questions!"

I tossed him the bottle and watched, horrified, as he proceeded to shove the exposed uterus back where it belonged — inside the cow. Talk about "making do!"

"Now go get that medicine and needle out of my pack. I'll just give her a shot of antibiotic."

He was quick and sure, kneeling beside the cow that was probably as shocked as I was. Coke bottle surgery!

"That oughta hold her a while." He got up and wiped his hands on his jeans. "But she'll probably have a hissy fit when I turn her lose, so get ready."

The big brown mama lumbered to her feet, looked around, bellowed, and left the country at a high lope. Buck swung up on his horse, grinning. "She'll be OK. I'll take a little weltie out here tomorrow to make sure."

The call was from the county sheriff's office.

"We've had a complaint about someone on your place. Is there somebody there named Buck?"

My heart sank. "What's he supposed to have done?"

"It seems he threatened your neighbors. A deputy is on the way."

Glenn said: "Let's find Buck and see what this is all about."

Buck looked at us and chuckled. "I told them, all right," he said. "Those people across the road, they fight in the middle of the night so loud I can't sleep. And I gotta get up at four to get to work. So I went and told them if they didn't quit, I'd wrap their legs around their necks so tight they'd be shouting up their own assholes."

Glenn, Starla, and I looked at each other with only one thought. We had to hide Buck.

"You go in the back bedroom, and don't you come out," I told him with all the authority of a mother who had raised two rambunctious sons. "You hear me?"

"Yes'm."

"I'll talk to the deputy," Glenn said. "Don't worry. Just stay back there and keep quiet."

But Starla and I were both worried and sat down in the living room like a pair of wax dolls to wait.

The deputy was a solid little man with eyes like buckshot. He listened as Glenn explained that Buck hadn't meant anything, and that the threat wasn't a serious matter.

We hadn't heard anything, but we certainly would take care of the problem.

Buck, his ear to the bedroom door, decided at that point he'd had enough and would fight his own battle. Down the hall he came!

"I'm just tryin' to earn a living, and those folks won't let me get a night's sleep. What would you know about it? You cops are all alike. Just yellow chicken shits."

I reached for a heavy brass candlestick ready to silence his big mouth. Starla clutched her hands tightly in her lap and managed to look sad and sullen both at the same time. The deputy stood still, eyes flickering, his hand resting on his pistol.

Glenn stepped between them, quieted Buck with a lethal glance, and explained Buck as well as anyone could, including repeating Buck's threat word for word.

At that point the deputy couldn't hide a smile. "Yes, well," he hesitated, groping for self-control, "you understand, we had to check it out. If it happens again, report them for disturbing the peace and you . . ." — with a finger at Buck — "you apologize and see you don't do it again. That's our job."

"You should be ashamed," I told Buck when the deputy had gone. "You could've ended up in jail, you and your big mouth."

He shrugged, but his eyes twinkled. "Been there. Done that."

Naturally. In his twenty-six years, Buck had done almost everything.

We'd been in our new house for a month, enjoying the peace and solitude, and I was, I remember, in a kind of daze, smitten by the beauty of mountains, the yellow pastures of autumn, the depths of a silence unlike any other I'd known.

I was awaiting publication of my first poetry collection and a collection of short fiction — corroboration of that fragile belief in self that had steadied me for so long, kept me going in spite of rejections and little support.

The harvest moon was up — enormous and orange — a pumpkin glowing in the sky, touching every bush and tree with pure light, and glancing off the mountains that seemed iridescent.

We had gone to bed early, but, close to midnight, I sat up, startled by what I thought was the glow of headlights in the driveway.

"There's someone here," I said, nudging Glenn.

"Who'd come at this hour?"

"I don't know, but somebody has."

He got out of bed and picked up his .45. "Let's just see about this."

Cautiously I peered out the window, and there, in front of me, was Buck, his grin splitting his face.

"Gawd damn we missed you!" he shouted, shattering the quiet. As always, in the truck bed as in a Gypsy wagon, were dogs, cats, ropes, saddles, boxes, all of his and Starla's few possessions. Once again, as we found out, Buck had been fired for talking smart to the ranch foreman.

"I told him. I just had to. He had to be stuck on a saddle with band-aids, and he couldn't rope a cow if he had six arms. Besides . . ." — Buck frowned, remembering — "he was just plain wolf ugly. I couldn't stand takin' orders comin' out of that face. So I figured we'd help you folks out a while. You got that old trailer back of the shed. It'll suit us fine."

Of course, they were welcome, both of them, itinerants, wanderers, friends. I loved Buck like a renegade son, full of himself and life, crazy but good-hearted, rolling along like a tumbleweed, with Starla dragging behind. And Starla was, without doubt, the most superb cook I have ever met.

Out of nothing more than neck bones, onions, garlic, vinegar, and who knows what else, she could create a meal fit for the French ambassador.

Every night while we were in the process of moving — driving two hundred miles with things too precious to trust to a moving company — Starla was in the kitchen grilling, barbecuing, stewing, turning out some of the best food we've ever eaten.

It is my hope that somewhere along the road she found her niche — in a diner, a truck stop, a café in the middle of nowhere — and is creating her banquets for those lucky enough to stop. She had the touch and the know-how, nothing short of genius.

Both she and Buck pitched in after they arrived, helping build a temporary shed for the horses, unpacking, and cooking. I was putting the final touches on a manuscript, and went to my new study every afternoon to revise and put all into shape.

Buck, of course, was fascinated by the process. He'd come to my door and peer over my shoulder — an act I've always detested — and after a minute would remark: "You sure can type fast! That's really something how you can do that!" Then he'd call to Starla, who had the wit to leave me alone. "Honey! Come on in here and be polite and watch Jane type!"

At which point the Muse and the determination disappeared, and I'd go into the living room, grinding my teeth but being, myself, polite.

Both Glenn and I sighed with relief when Buck found a job up in Aravaipa and took off, leaving Starla behind — "Just till I get settled."

Oddly, she and I got along — or perhaps not so oddly, for she, too, was an original — an abused half-breed child, an unwed mother-to-be, the companion of a charming ne'er-do-well whom she happened to love. I think. Sometimes she looked at him as if she'd like to take a knife to his throat.

Certainly the West produces strange matings — matches between drifters and loners, cowboys and females looking for excitement or anything at all rather than staying single. I've seen it happen over and over — a woman panicked without a man, and the man of her choice a complete loser.

Not that Buck was that. He was honest, straightforward, and competent at what he knew, and certainly no abuser of women, regardless of his earlier failed marriages. Besides that, Starla was bound and determined to make something out of him. I hope she did.

A month went by. It was almost Thanksgiving. Buck was still gone, still trying to find a place for them to live.

The phone rang. "Will you accept a collect call from Buck?"

"You still typin' those books?" was the first thing out of his mouth.

"Yes." And quite happily without his help.

"I got Thanksgiving off. Can I come down and spend it with you folks?"

"You come," I told him. Then added: "God damn, we miss you!"

I did the turkey and my special wild rice, ham, mushroom and bourbon stuffing. Starla did the pies — sweet potato and pumpkin — both of which I detest, but thought if she made them I'd take at least a bite.

Buck arrived in his usual whirlwind, his Heeler dogs riding in the truck bed, tails waving, happy to be reunited with ours. Over an early dinner, he entertained us as usual with his tales, laughter, and teasing. Also with complaints.

"It's dry up there," he commented. "Haven't had rain in so long I forget what it's like." And to Glenn: "I want you to beat that drum of yours and make something happen."

241

Glenn can, indeed, beat his drum and summon rain. I've seen him do it, and so have a number of others. The fact that no one — not neighbors, ranchers, shop-keepers, or cowboys — sees anything ridiculous in the sight of a six-foot-four man banging on a drum and dancing, illustrates the vast difference between East and West. We believe in doing whatever it takes.

One of my funniest memories is of the evening when Jesús came in from an inspection of our pasture, looking glum. Seeing me, he came over and showed me the dry and withered grass he'd picked. *"Muy malo,"* he had said. "Tell Meester Glenn to make *tambor.*"

With much laughter, I had relayed the message, and Glenn got out of his chair. "I'll do it."

Within minutes, he had been two-stepping up the driveway, beating and chanting, while Jesús had stood solemnly by, nodding his approval, one sandaled foot keeping time.

Of course, it had rained. How could it not?

After dinner, after Starla's pies had been devoured as the delicacies they were, Glenn picked up his drum and went out. Soon we heard him singing, felt the beat of the old

Indian drum through the walls of the house.

Buck slapped his leg and stomped one booted foot. "That'll do it!" he said just as he left on his drive back.

By ten o'clock rain was pattering on our roof. I was curled in a chair when the phone rang.

"Will you accept . . . ?"

"Yes," I said.

"Gawd damn."

"What's the matter?" I had visions of Buck, his truck wrecked in some unnamed cañon.

"He still beatin' that drum?"

I laughed. "No, but it's raining."

Buck gave a snort. "Well, it's rainin' up here like a cow pissin' on a flat rock. Tell him to quit."

Glenn said: "And tell him I hit the snow side by accident, so he'd better watch out."

"Sure he did," was Buck's comment.

But in yet another collect call the next day, we heard that it had, indeed, snowed some six inches. "Gawd damn," Buck kept saying with a kind of awe in his voice. "Well, Gawd damn."

Naturally, in the middle of December, came the word that Buck had, once again, lost his job.

"But I've got another in Amarillo. Drivin'

trucks," he said as he loaded up his own.

"You'll hate it," I told him. "There's no mountains in Amarillo."

"We want you to come to the wedding," Starla said. "I'll let you know when."

Of course, we never made it to the wedding. Finding a house, horse, and dog sitter made leaving impossible. But I missed them, even though I relished my writing time.

Just last week I said to Glenn: "I bet Buck shows up again someday."

He rolled his eyes. "Like a bad penny. I'll be happy if I never see him again."

"You know," I said, "I loved Buck. He was like my son."

"God help you," came the answer.

But for all of his failings and bluster, Buck was fun — a beam of sunlight that couldn't be captured, only enjoyed while it lasted. Here today, gone tomorrow may be his motto, but my blessings go with him on the long trail.

Pale Horse, Pale Rider

Buck left behind a token — a Red Heeler pup, one of an abused litter he'd discovered and swiped. The only pup he couldn't catch to take with him was a tiny red male with haunted eyes that dug himself a burrow under the shed and refused to come out.

"He's all yours," Buck said, and stomped off to his old truck already loaded beyond its capacity, while I made a resolution — to tame and rescue the cowering creature that had been hurt and shamed beyond its puppy capacity.

Within a few days, the pup that wasn't more than three months old was showing up for breakfast and dinner which I left near to his bolt hole. I always made sure I was there, close, but not so close as to frighten him, and talking my usual nonsense, getting him used to the sound of an unhostile voice.

After a month, he would come out into the yard. After two months, he began to follow me, sometimes attempting to "heel" me according to his nature. I'd be working in the garden and feel a cold nose at my ankle, but if I turned too quickly, the little dog would dash to a safe distance and watch me with those sad, dark eyes. It was progress of a sort, but all the time I was cursing whoever had brutalized a helpless creature, and Glenn was doing the same. To him, there is no greater sin than abuse of animals or humans, and so he left me to my task.

Patience. It takes an endless supply with an animal that has been taught to distrust people. I'd learned that first with Rascal, an Irish Setter that I adopted and, gradually, made into a loyal and constant companion. And I'd learned it with Jefe, that, I deduced from his actions, had at one time been beaten within an inch of his life. Even now, after years, I am always careful to act the same around him, never making a quick move, but this has paid off in a splendid relationship that had made us both happy.

The day came when I put out a hand and petted the little dog. He almost purred — before he ran away. I didn't push it, only did the same thing the next day and the next, and the day after that.

Time passed. I could sit on the porch steps, and he would come and sit beside me, quivering in delight as I stroked him and talked my nonsense.

He was a fine dog — alert and intelligent

— and at last the day came when I picked him up and carried him onto the porch where he lay in my lap as if he knew he belonged, listening to our easy conversation, his head turning from one to the other in an effort to join in.

It was a happy evening, and I was full of the feeling of accomplishment, as Glenn and I tossed potential names back and forth.

"Let's let him choose," I said finally.

"And he will." Glenn leaned over and stroked the soft head, the velvet ears, and the little dog closed his eyes and snuggled deeper into my lap. He was home. At last.

I didn't see him the next morning, which wasn't unusual, as he still spent most of his time in his burrow under the shed. He'd come out when he was ready. But, as I drove out the gate on my way to get the mail, I saw him at the edge of the road.

Why is he sleeping there? I wondered.

And then I knew. If whoever had run him down had shown up at that moment, I would have killed him, attacked with fists, teeth, nails, and anger so intense that I screamed with it.

Someone had murdered a loving heart, taken a life that had just begun. Someone, carelessly and perhaps with deliberation, had destroyed faith.

★ ★ ★

We had been here almost eight years when Dolf, the dark chocolate, blanket Appaloosa, developed an abscessed hoof.

Dolf, one of the most intelligent animals either of us had ever known, had one serious problem. He hated any horse but Jefe. Dolf would think, plan how to kill every new horse we brought on the place, with a diabolical kind of cleverness.

If we happened to leave a stall open and a new and innocent horse wandered in, Dolf knew it, had been waiting for his opportunity, often for as long as five months. Once the new horse was inside, Dolf would come in behind, pin the unsuspecting newcomer to the wall, and proceed to kick the stuffing out of him, giving no mercy.

Luckily several times I heard the fighting and stopped Dolf from half killing or crippling Doc. But at last we'd had enough. As a saddle horse, Dolf was splendid. A grandmother or a three-year-old could ride him in safety, even bareback with a rope and a halter. It was only with other horses that he was dangerous.

So we lent him to a local dude ranch, knowing he could mother kids but couldn't, as a newcomer himself, take on an entire string of dude horses. Of course, he didn't.

What he did, eventually, was rip his hoof and pastern in barb wire — the curse of all horses. What the ranch boss did was doctor the injury himself without the help of a competent vet. On the surface, Dolf appeared to have healed and, when the ranch was sold, was returned home to us.

We were glad to have him back. He was, despite his problem, a fine horse and part of our own early love affair. But in a few months, the trouble began. The torn foot had never truly healed. The infection stayed deep inside his hoof, and finally broke out again.

We called the vet, treated him for months, soaking the leg, wrapping the hoof, giving shots of antibiotic, and hoping. But Dolf kept losing weight. Looking at him made me want to weep — the bony hips, the shoulders like slabs of rock, the ribs that showed too plainly.

But he was game. He fought, and so did we, cutting up apples, carrots, celery, watermelons, dosing his food with vitamins, all the while remembering Jesús saying: *"Muy malo."*

Had he known something we hadn't? Was he prescient? I'll never know, although Glenn says that Jesús did, indeed, foresee the end with the intuitive knowledge of one who had lived close to the land and animals all his life.

The day came when I called Tom, the vet, and Victor, who services the district with his back hoe — for ditches, tanks, and graves. The appointment was made. Victor arrived with a rumble at six in the morning and dug his hole — eight feet deep.

Tom came early. Glenn was in the shower. "Don't worry," I said. "You don't have to watch. I'll do it."

Then, determined, I marched out, haltered Dolf, and led him behind the barn to stand beside the deep hole in the ground. And at that point my courage failed. I had watched dogs go to their maker, but Dolf was a part of our history. I had ridden him, loved him from the first. I had laughed like a fool when, riding him, he pulled his favorite trick — jumping ten feet sideways while at a high lope — laughed and stayed on.

"Tom," I said, "you do it. I can't watch." I put my arms around Dolf's big neck, stroked his velvet nose, and whispered in his ear. *"Vaya con Dios, amigo."* Then I turned and ran past the barn where Jefe, Amos, and Peanut, psychic, as all horses are psychic, had their heads thrust over their gates, ears up, eyes wild. They whinnied, and the sound was the echo of my tears.

Glenn came hurrying from the house, and I said: "No. Don't go. It's too late. It's over."

And it was.

In Search of . . .

This year the summer rains came early — in June — and then stopped. July stretches out, hot and dry, and grass that had turned green and gone to seed is withered. Even the ubiquitous careless weed droops in pastures and along the lane, and my garden sulks, all energy going into sustaining life instead of into production.

I grow short-tempered as every day clouds build, then dissipate. *What's the use?* I ask myself, dragging hoses to shriveled plants. Why am I doing this? I'm caught in an endless circle of chores like a gerbil in a cage, tramping between house, gardens, and barn in a routine that never varies.

Riding is out of the question. It would be torture for both horse and rider in weather like this. As it is, the horses stand in the pond cooling their hoofs, splashing their bellies, and now and then actually rolling, their heads held high above the water.

Worse, my mother, who is ninety-one, has had a series of strokes, small and large, and I've had to move her from the retirement community in Tucson that she loved to a nursing home and then to a local assisted-living home, all of which, in her eyes, is my fault. Guilt, deserved or not, sits on my shoulders like a shroud.

Glenn and I clean out the apartment where she has lived so happily for the last eight years. Every drawer, every closet is stuffed full of paper — canceled checks from the 1940s, old diplomas, letters from friends I remember from childhood, every birthday and Christmas card received for a decade. All this interspersed with plastic grocery bags, unused stationery, Christmas wrapping paper, used and new, photographs of long-dead relatives, some I don't recognize.

I want to call it junk, except to her it is precious, a record of many lives intertwined. Two days is not enough to sort through ninety years.

When the movers bring the chests, desk, and bureau to the house, I take my time, put keepsakes aside in a safe place, attempt to think myself into my mother's head and retain what, to her, is important — letters written by my father, notebooks containing poetry she wrote as a student, all my grade school report cards, birth certificates, and her own father's naturalization papers. I save these things for myself, for her, and for my children, a little history of our own.

From first-hand experience I know the importance of family papers. When, in 1989, my agent suggested that I write a novel, I was stunned. What I'd published up until then was poetry and short stories. A novel seemed beyond my ability until Glenn said to me that evening: "I have all this information on Big Nose Kate that I'm not going to do anything with. Take it. There's a great novel in her life."

That night he handed me several thick files containing interviews he'd done with her family, photographs, letters she herself had written, and articles written and published by Glenn with Professor A. W. Bork, who had actually interviewed her before she died at the Arizona Pioneer's Home in 1940.

As I read, I realized that a true heroine had been, from the first, blackballed — that an intelligent and sophisticated woman had been defamed in print and on film, simply because no one had taken the time to do the research.

On Kate's behalf, I got mad. And madder still when Glenn related the story about how he had been misled by a so-called "famous" historian who lied to him saying that Kate had died in California when, in fact, he knew she had died in Arizona. By the time Glenn discovered the truth and was in touch with the Arizona Pioneer's Home and with her niece and nephew, they had moved from a house into a trailer and, out of necessity, had thrown out or burned all of Kate's letters.

For any historian this is a tragedy, but fortunately Hattie Maddox and Albert Horony had long memories. They knew quite well who their "Aunt Mary" was, what she had done, where she had been. They remembered visiting her in Dos Cabezas, Arizona, and they remembered her visiting them as children on their homestead near Glenwood Springs where Doc Holliday died.

History lives in memories, in diaries, letters, oral testimony. As I sort through papers, I keep this in mind. History repeats. The future leans on the past.

As I delved into the known facts of Big Nose Kate's life, the frontier West came alive. She became my guide, my voice, much as Geronimo had been.

I wrote — and felt she was looking over my shoulder. I liked her — her toughness, her background, her early education in the courts of emperors. Here was a woman who had been trashed by writers who hadn't even known her name, and a proud name it was. Mary Catherine Horony, born in Budapest to a family of minor nobility.

By contrast, Mattie Earp for whom I'd searched in vain in 1986, faded like a worn piece of gingham. At last I had a real person, a woman I knew in my bones, whose voice I could almost hear as I wrote. Together Glenn and I did follow-up research — in Albany, Griffin, Breckenridge, Texas, in Las Vegas and Santa Fé, New Mexico. Thanks to Glenn, who once again became my tour guide, I saw more of Texas than I knew existed — Palo Duro Cañon, Amarillo, the Staked Plains, Fort Davis, Borracho Springs. We drove and drove for uncounted miles, stopping in small towns where the only motels had outer doors that didn't lock, or bathrooms reached only by crawling over the bed, in dry counties where, simply to have a beer with dinner after a hard day, we paid large fees to join the local club. We drove, and I learned, loving every second of the journey. Beyond the car windows was the land that had seen Kiowas and Comanches, buffalo, the U.S. cavalry, the Mexican War, the noise and dust of hundreds of thousands of longhorn cattle headed up the Western Cattle Trail.

And I made a decision — one that will echo forever in my memory. I said: "You know, I can't write about all this just looking out a car window. If Kate and Doc rode the trail, I need to do it, too."

From somewhere came the unrestrained sound of Kate's laughter egging me on.

Glenn never flinched. He said: "Fine. We'll go back for Jefe and see what you can do."

And so began the adventure of a lifetime, a ride from Griffin to Vernon, Texas, a last furious sprint across the Red River into what was, in Kate's and Doc's time, Indian Territory, ten days of living what had, to me, been only legend. I learned the rise and fall of the land, the groves of pecans and hackberries by the creeks, the buzz of the long-tailed flycatchers, the bursting of Texas bluebonnets that turned an entire journey into a trip over fallen sky.

It's rolling country — that part of the Western Cattle Trail north of Griffin — dotted with rock outcroppings, covered with low-growing buffalo grass. The wind is constant, the yucca and cactus miniature versions of those farther west, and always the horizon draws farther away.

After a day or two, a kind of lightheadedness came over me, a sense of freedom like I'd never felt. I started to laugh and couldn't stop, and Jefe flicked his ears at me as if to ask what the joke was. I patted his neck. "We're free, babe," I said. "It's just you and me and a thousand miles of nothing."

I felt his answer in the sudden tensing of his body. In him was the blood of mustang ancestors, a wildness that matched my own. He wanted to run, to do what he understood best, with the wind driving him on. I let him into the smooth lope that he could keep up for miles without breaking into a sweat. Had anyone been around, they'd have wondered at the sight — a woman on a spotted horse laughing her head off for no apparent reason, jumping fences and trespassing without permission, and not giving a damn.

The fact that what I was doing was dangerous never entered my head on those long days. Thinking back, it seems foolish, a crazy notion that succeeded perhaps because it was meant to, because I learned more about myself in those ten days than I had in all the years previously, and I think that the same held true for Kate — on the lam for setting Griffin on fire and breaking the man she loved out of jail.

That was a rainy spring. All the rivers — the Clear Fork of the Brazos, the Double

Mountain Fork of the Brazos, the Wichita — were in flood, roiling red torrents of water and soil that even I, in the grip of magic, didn't attempt to cross.

Each morning Glenn and I checked the maps, met by pre-arrangement beside each river, the only problem with that being that Jefe hated trailers and balked at being loaded, a process that often took forty-five minutes of coaxing, cajoling, and at last pulling and shoving him inside. It never got easier through repetition, and at some point I swore I'd never again own a horse that wouldn't load.

Cussing him helped the most. He seemed to understand the moment when our tempers were stretched to the breaking point and the air around us turned blue, causing Glenn to say: "Now you know why mule skinners had a string of cusswords."

Whatever works.

The plains affect me like tonic. Here the Red River, spread out in bottomland, beckons, lures, conjures up scenes from history and Hollywood.

I am John Wayne riding point; behind me, three thousand head of longhorns make the earth tremble. I am all the unnamed cowboys headed up the trail, and I am Big

Nose Kate and Doc Holliday riding for their lives, headed into adventure. I am also a woman I'm just beginning to know — a stranger unafraid of people, empty spaces, or the deceptive flowing of one of the mightiest of rivers.

Jefe dances under me, and snatches at the bit. Over the last days, we've become part of one another, and now he reads my mind. We're going to run this river for the excitement of it, because it dares us, because, in the words of Sir Edmund Hilary about Everest: "It is there."

Glenn, too, reads my thoughts and says: "You're crazy."

"Maybe."

He looks out, studies the water, the pale fingers of sandbars, false promises in the midst of terra-cotta water. The river here near old Doan's Crossing isn't confined between high banks but stretches across a broad flood plain.

"You might hit quicksand," he tells me. "So if you're going, do it fast, and God bless."

Jefe snorts agreement. Fast is what he loves, and unlike many desert-bred horses he has no fear of water.

I tighten the tie-down on my hat, bend over for a kiss. "I'll be fine," I assure Glenn, knowing that it's true, and knowing, too, that this man I married will always urge me on, stand behind me, and wish me success.

Jefe and I maneuver down the sandy bank that crumbles under us so he squats on his haunches. His heart begins to pound as we reach the bottom and I give him his head. Rearing back, he then propels himself forward with powerful hind legs, and we're running with the wind in our faces, the sound of his hoofs in our ears.

He hits the water with a grunt, shattering the surface into splinters of glass, but he doesn't slow until he's belly-deep. Even then, he thrusts on, snorting, accepting the challenge like the splendid creature he is.

For us the crossing takes only minutes. With a herd of unruly longhorns the process must have seemed interminable to the trail drivers. Some of the cows would have refused, some would have fought, while others bogged down and had to be roped and pulled. Trailing cattle was hard, dangerous, dirty work, but not without compensation. Always there was the land that struck even the most jaded eye with its beauty. Always the sense of accomplishment, of having proved one's self against formidable odds.

And Big Nose Kate and Doc — what was

it they felt on their desperate ride — man and woman alone, reduced to minutiae by thousands of miles of magnificence?

They left no record, but I think I know. I think that, in spite of basic differences, they came to recognize that they were rebels and reckless, taking advantage of the moment, possessed of the courage necessary to beat the odds.

I think that their love and the rest of their lives were shaped and rooted in the journey across the plains, and that, like me, they always held sacred the magic of place, the music of wind and bird song, freedom that broke their hearts then put them together again stronger, larger than before.

I know because that is what happened to me.

The Earps and More

Inevitably, as I followed in Big Nose Kate's footsteps, I learned more about the Earps and Tombstone's supporting players, both good and bad, than I thought possible.

We were on our first trip, somewhere in West Texas, when Glenn said: "I've always wanted to go see Steve McLaury. Now's my chance."

"Who's he?"

"Frank and Tom's grandnephew. He's just up the road a ways in Oklahoma."

Once again I was intrigued by the fact that historical figures have living relatives and descendants, that history need not be the boring, one-dimensional subject our books and educational system have made it, but can be as alive, as fascinating as anything told to me by Archie, Edith, Buck or by any one of a hundred old-timers that I've known. Out of nowhere that afternoon came a nephew of the two McLaurys who were killed at the famous gunfight at the OK Corral.

As always, Glenn had the map in his head,

and the country beckoned. And, since childhood, when every morning on the way to school I sat enthralled at the railroad crossing and read the names on the sides of the passing cars, I've had an itchy foot.

Those names are gone, the magic replaced, the logos painted out, but I remember them — **The Way of the Zephyrs, The Cotton Belt, The Route of the Phoebe Snow,** the great Spanish Cross that symbolized the Santa Fé — and the shining rails a magic carpet, the road to adventure.

"What are we waiting for?" I asked.

Glenn phoned Steve and set up a time and a place to meet, and we drove north toward the Wichita Mountains — Kiowa country, home of Satanta and Kicking Bird, the place immortalized by Scott Momaday as "Rainy Mountain."

I remembered his description, repeated it to myself. "To look upon that landscape . . . is to lose your sense of proportion. Your imagination comes to life, and this, you think, is where Creation was begun."

I have been in many such places — on the High Plains, in the Chiricahuas, and in Monument Valley in the midst of storm. Creation could have begun in any one of these, with no one to bear witness. At times, however, I think that the moment of Creation replicates itself in every morning, every silence, every sighting of bird, flower, horse, thundercloud. In even the smallest is the beginning of the world, the moment of our birth, the shocking brilliance of an interior explosion that can only be called epiphany.

On our journey it was raining, and the mountains were green, almost luminous behind a floating scarf of mist and drizzle. Like a blurred watercolor, the land surrounded us, and it was then that I understood the ecstasy of creation and its opposite — the agony of severance from all that is loved. The sorrow, the longing of the original inhabitants who had been removed and placed on reservations, became a reality, a bitter taste in my mouth. How they must have longed for home, where softly rounded hills rise up from the plain, where the prairie, in spring, is a tapestry of grass and flowers, and the summer heat shimmers in blue waves above yellow grass.

"I feel bad," I said, looking out and into the past.

"About what?"

"The Indians. Imagine how they felt, having to leave a home like this."

He sighed and nodded agreement, but his answer was that of a life-long student of history and human nature. "Don't blame yourself. That's what we all seem to do best these days. But there have always been Cæsars."

Of course, I knew this. The armies of the strong have always overcome those of the weak, but it does not make loss and separation any easier. It does not make the past heroic but merely fact, a part of the flowing of what we, perhaps mistakenly, call civilization.

We met Steve McLaury, his wife, Peg, and son, Shane, for lunch, and the conversation at first was about everything but Steve's uncles and their part in Tombstone's violent history. Steve was a lawyer, as is Shane, and both had lived their lives and practiced in the town where they and their forebears were born.

The land and its history shaped them, as it shapes all of us. They were smart, shrewd, cautious men of the plains, devoted to family and to their roots.

My observation was proved correct when, as Glenn and I got up and were saying our good byes after lunch, Steve grinned and said: "Come on out to the house. I wasn't so sure about you, so I decided we'd meet here first so I could look you over."

Shane grinned, too, adding: "And if he hadn't liked you, he'd have said so long."

The afternoon spun away. We moved from Steve and Peg's white clapboard house to the law office, looking at old photographs — replaying the aftermath of the famous gunfight, when Steve's grandfather, Will, arrived in Arizona Territory seeking revenge for the death of his brothers, Frank and Tom.

About his father Steve remarked: "He was the most stable of the McLaurys back then."

"Meaning?"

He picked up a photograph of Frank wearing a straw boater and looking like a gambler and a ladies' man. "Well," he said, "my father didn't spend his whole life holding a grudge like Will and the rest. He had better things to do." He chuckled. "A funny thing. Will brought Frank's pistol back. We had it around for years, and never thought about it till some cowhand dropped it in the river. We never did find it."

Several years later we read in the paper that Frank McLaury's pistol had been "discovered" in a trunk in someone's attic and was being offered for sale — "to serious bidders only" — for as I recall, several hundred thousand dollars.

"Do you think they dragged the river?" I asked Glenn with a laugh.

He gave me a look. "As P. T. Barnum once said . . . 'There's a sucker born every minute.' People believe what they want to believe."

Given the tangled web that has been spun around Tombstone, the Earps, their wives, mistresses, enemies, and friends, I, myself, believe that.

Do Not Go Gently

Everyone I talk to seems to be facing the problem of aging parents, which is not one problem but many, the worst of which, aside from dealing with the bureaucracy, are the personality changes that occur with aging and the disintegration of mind and body.

Although in retrospect I was aware of this, I was in no way prepared for the extent of my mother's anger and the rage she has turned on me. I have become not only a child again and guilty for sins I have not committed, but a mother figure that can do nothing right, partly, as I have come to understand, with my own permission.

The entire summer has come and gone without my notice. Chores have been done by rote, with none of the usual pleasure, none of the moments of seeing that are at the root of my being. Instead, I have been flagellating myself for being a monster child. I have been running on the precarious edge of losing self in a hopeless attempt to please another.

Words, which heretofore have always

come in a flood, falter, as the vital connection with self and surroundings is intruded upon, erased by a sense of duty. Coming to terms with the fact that this sense has swelled out of proportion has been the most difficult task of my life, an obstacle looming many times larger than that of leaving my first marriage and striking out on my own.

In my mother's mind, I have abandoned her to desolation. Not true, of course, but finding a decent and affordable assisted-living home meant moving her from the fairy tale retirement complex in Tucson to a place closer to us.

It is only after many months that, on the verge of collapse, I begin to question my motives — and hers — and why my response has been so hysterical.

For one raised to please — and to do so unselfishly — the withholding of praise or the faintest hint of criticism is both wound and spur. If I have failed, it must be due to a lack in myself, and therefore I must try harder. This is an attitude ingrained in me and in many women of my generation, and one that I feel must not only be recognized, but placed into the proper perspective. It is also the attitude that permitted me, and thousands of others, to accept undeserved and often criminal forms of abuse. The use of guilt to induce obedience is pernicious, and yet how often it is wielded — by religion, by parents, by educators, and, tragically, by husbands and wives.

The stitches, the threads that bind mothers and daughters are many, some too small to be seen, some so common they are easily overlooked or ignored. Still, patterns, good or bad, innocent or knowing, exist, and are often astonishingly similar for all of us.

For weeks now, I have been mapping my own state of mind and that of my mother's. Glenn says: "You've done your best. Stop torturing yourself, or you'll have a breakdown."

He is right, of course, but to end the torture I had to follow what I felt to the source, to recognize that, for many, aging and the certainty of death, the terror of abandonment bring out needs and traits that previously were hidden, and that suffering begets more suffering. I therefore had the choice in once again participating in abuse of self — the Pavlovian response taught to me as a child and continued for the years of my first marriage — or of standing away, refusing to permit another, even my own mother, to reduce me to non-life.

This morning I got up early and went out

to feed horses. The sun edged over the tawny tops of the Peloncillos, bringing cañons and crevices to sudden prominence. A faint breeze came out of the southwest, and it was cool, a harbinger of fall. Over the surface of the pond, a hawk skimmed, followed by his reflection, and from behind the barn came the barking of quail.

How splendid it all was! How perfect in its newness! I opened the gate and was welcomed by nickers from the horses who sorted themselves out and went into their stalls.

For a moment I stood facing the wind, breathing the scents of dried grass, the elusive fragrance of a secret blooming. After a dark journey, I had come alive again, stronger than before, and I thought of those who had confided their anguish over their parents to me — the woman whose mother was delusional and obsessed with her vanished beauty; the writer whose father, in a rage, smashed the furniture in his nursing home; the daughter whose parent accused her of attempted murder — and wished I could comfort and advise them.

"Do your best," I would tell them, "but do not forget to savor the world. Do your best, but remember that selfishness is not the sin we were brought up to believe. Take care of self first, for only then can we care for others."

Death comes to us all, but life is precious, and we must take delight in it, give thanks for it while we can, and let our hearts and minds guide us in the steps of its dance.

Above all else, it is the silence in these lonely valleys that I love — as tonight when I went at dusk to let horses out and stopped, and stood, and listened to nothing at all. Not wind, not cricket scrape, not the music of birds that had all gone to roost. On the path a garter snake — black, striped vivid yellow — moved away in its sinuous motion but made no sound, not even when it reached the shelter of dry weeds and vanished, a twisting shadow.

It has been my observation that silence is actually made up of a thousand small murmurings, but tonight there were none. Stillness was absolute. For a long while I stood, tasting the warm night air, while Tomás, the orange cat with eyes of translucent jade wound between my legs, and I thought of that silence such as this is both prayer and blessing, and that I had been away from both too long.

When I came back to the house, I was filled with music — the music that ultimately gives birth to language — and once again the question of the Muse tantalized. Who, or what, is it that inspires, that comes and just as quickly vanishes, leaving us in thrall?

May Sarton, whom I knew and corresponded with for many years, and who very kindly gave me praise in her book, *Endgame*, and in the form of a jacket blurb for *No Roof But Sky*, was adamant that the Muse is always female. For her this was certainly true. For me the Muse is often what can only be called a hovering in the air, an intangible wave that dazzles, then is gone, leaving me shaken, driven to find release in the form of language.

Silence. Time. Solitude. These three necessities have been lacking in my life. The Muse does not care for trivia or daily paperwork, for phone calls that involve listening to endless "menus," and pushing the correct button, for dealing with government agencies to which I am nothing more than an anonymous nuisance.

All of this conspired to build a wall that the Muse refused to climb. But tonight — and earlier this morning — place itself shattered the barrier and permitted the Muse to enter.

For a writer, not being able to write over

an extended period is a severance from life, a breakdown of existence, a sensual loss that leaves that person bereft, incapable of action.

When I moved from my trance, when I once again took time to stroke the offered soft noses and stood with my arm over Jefe's warm back, I understood where I had been, how far from grace I had traveled.

My roots, my source lie here, in the silence, in the shadow of the mountains, in the garden that, as every fall, is bursting with the fruits of summer, with thousands of roses that scent the air, the purple globes of eggplants beneath furred leaves, pomegranates that, like huge rubies, bend branches with their weight.

These are the fruits of Persia, the fruits of love, proof positive of life and the joy that exist if only we will open our eyes and see.

The Muses

The girl-woman with wild auburn hair and the skittishness of a wary doe came to the table where Glenn and I were having breakfast in the Rodeo Store.

Breathlessly she apologized for intruding. "I just . . . I just wanted to thank you for your poetry," she said. "I've read *No Roof But Sky* over and over."

She backed away then. On impulse I got up and followed her. "Who are you?" I asked.

"I'm a poet, too." She stood still, watching me with bright eyes before she went on in a rush. "I'd like to send you a manuscript to thank you. Would you mind? It's OK to say no."

There is nothing sadder than to receive a badly written, poor excuse for a manuscript, for then the burden of lying and giving false hope, or telling the truth and damning another's belief becomes a millstone that crushes two people. Still, I could not disappoint this woman who appeared so fragile and yet so certain of herself. I gave her my address.

Four days later the manila envelope arrived, and I went to my desk to read. After one stanza I was feeling what my novelist friend, Zeke Browning, describes as "the chills."

I went out to the breakfast room where Glenn was having toast and coffee. "Read this," I said. "Tell me what you think."

He grimaced. "Do I have to? Is it that bad?"

"Just read it."

After a few minutes he looked up. "This is extraordinary."

"I know," I said, and vowed in that instant to help this stranger who was no longer a stranger but a full-fleshed friend and equal.

To my delight I learned that Victoria and her husband, Phil, had bought a house high on the slope of our mountains. As yet, it was a weekend home, but simply having a similar spirit close by and being able to spend Sunday afternoons talking about poetry and the threads that combine to write a poem shook me awake.

I felt I had opened a door into a room I'd never seen or had forgotten. Cautiously I wrote a few poems of my own. But I was in the middle of a novel, a sequel to my first

Big Nose Kate novel, and, for me, prose and poetry cannot mix. Still, that unfurnished room was waiting in my head.

In the spring I was asked to give the keynote lecture at the Cochise College Writing Celebration, and, of course, I accepted. Then I asked Victoria to come along, bringing her three exquisite manuscripts. Maybe, I thought, just maybe we would find another who recognized what she had achieved and could help her to publish.

If Victoria had opened doors, Diane Freund, whose memoir class we sat in on, broke down walls — not only for me but for all who were there that afternoon.

I watched women, and men, discover themselves through the power of memory. I watched as some wept and others grew thoughtful. And I watched as Victoria rediscovered a talent and a life.

Since that day she has been submitting her work and writing an extraordinary memoir. Since that day I have begun a third manuscript of poetry. And, far more important, the three of us — all women who have lived, loved, suffered, triumphed — have become a unit, each a source of inspiration for the other.

So, in a way, May Sarton was correct. The shared experiences of women can give birth to ideas, and books, and a kind of love that transcends the physical and dwells in the realm of inspiration. And always, every meeting, every conversation, causes us to look with astonishment at the gifts that have been given us.

Grandma Price and

a Passel of Pups

One of my favorite characters from Cochise County history is the woman affectionately known as Grandma Price.

The story goes that, in 1903, she and her husband came to Turkey Creek to homestead, and, when he deserted her and their ten children and one orphaned nephew, Grandma hitched up her skirts and went to work. She not only preserved the original homestead, but prospered, acquiring land of her own and becoming a woman of substance. Further, regardless of abandonment and the trials of running a ranch on her own, she raised her entire brood to adulthood, surely a model for today's single mothers.

The only photograph of Grandma Price I've seen shows her as an old woman wearing a man's work boots, apron, and tattered dress. A sunbonnet shields her worn and leathery face — the face of an indomitable survivor. She is puffing on a corncob pipe, which, to me, says all I need to know about her character. This was a woman who served no master, who relied on herself, and be damned to convention or what the neighbors might have thought. In short, she is my kind of woman.

She and this photo were the inspiration for one of my favorite stories, "Aunt Addy and the Cattle Rustler." I've had a soft spot for Grandma ever since.

Perhaps it is not coincidence that one of the women who owns the assisted-living home where my mother is staying is Grandma's great granddaughter and named for her — Molly Price.

Molly is a handsome woman with a mop of curly, graying hair and startling dark blue eyes as filled with energy as her ancestor's, devoted and fiercely protective of those she calls "my old ones."

Obviously these traits of energy, efficiency, and dedication must run in the family, for on one of my first visits Molly mentioned a litter of pups that had just been born to a stray her son had rescued. He had been driving down a street in Tucson when he saw another driver stop and kick out a dog. Horrified, he, too, stopped, found the victim — a pregnant female — and brought her to Molly. Within weeks, eleven puppies were whelped.

"We'll take two," I said after visiting the newborns in their box, and regardless of the fact that I have always preferred purebred dogs.

It was impossible to tell what had gone into the breeding of the pups, although the mother appeared to have a good deal of boxer in her mixed with hound. Most importantly, however, she had a sweet temperament, which we hoped would pass to her offspring.

The problem Glenn and I have, living in relative isolation, is that we need several dogs, both inside and out, as a simple precaution, and, while our two Mastiffs provide protection, we had gotten down to only one aging and very deaf "yard" dog.

In addition to all the approved reasons, we are, both of us, what is known as "dog simple," which is the same as being "horse simple," a disease one is born with and which leads to the adoption of every stray and waif that crosses our paths.

Now, being the proud owners of two pups, I said: "They need their parvo and distemper shots."

Glenn shook his head. "We'll have to do all eleven. It's not fair just to do two and let the rest go."

Except there was a hitch when Molly pointed out that, being licensed by the state, she cannot accept anything that might be construed as a gift or bribe.

Glenn thought a minute. "That's fine," he said, his eyes twinkling. "I'll just buy them all."

Molly looked startled. "All?"

"Yep."

And so it was that the pups received their shots. Molly and her family kept five, and ultimately we arrived home with six wriggling bodies in the back of the truck — five females and one alert little male that Glenn named Highbeam, a name that has become famous in our house.

When my son Dan was a student at Rutgers, he and four friends lived in a condo on the edge of the ghetto. Dan, being outgoing, immediately made friends with his black neighbors, including the local pimp, Highbeam Jackson. We have spent many an evening laughing over the exploits of Highbeam as related by Dan, who is a born mimic and storyteller.

Dan and Highbeam, the pup, took one look at each other and fell in love, and three days ago the pup flew with his new friend to Phoenix where he has his own dog run, outdoor igloo, and indoor bed, and puppy treats, and where he will be spoiled to death.

Now Glenn and I begin the task of training five girls to "Come," "Sit," "Stay," and "Heel" on leash. Yard dogs or not, for their own safety, they must learn the basics.

Thus far, what they have learned is that lap time is best of all, and treats can be had if they come when called; that leashes exist to be bitten and tugged on; and that life in the wide open space of the dog yard with its pine trees, tall grass, and assortment of chew toys is a never-ending journey of discovery.

No Room in the Inn

I am talking to a woman whom I know slightly, and she asks if we've had much trouble with "illegal aliens," that being the new term for those previously called "wetbacks." It is a term that I find irritating, for the word "alien" always conjures a picture of little green men in a space ship and not the thousands of humans from across the Mexican border who, in desperate need of work, attempt to cross into the United States.

"No," I tell her. "Our two Mastiffs tend to keep people away."

That is fact. Cisco, the fawn male with his fierce black mask, weighs two hundred and forty, and Ling-Ling, the black-brindle female is no lightweight. Neither, however, is an inveterate killer, and neither has to be. Potential trespassers take one look and go elsewhere. Wisely so, for both dogs have been bred to protect under any circumstance.

The woman says: "You're lucky. We've had a stream of them all summer. Last week

I had a man and his wife carrying a nursing baby right in my front yard." She tosses her head, then smirks self-righteously. "I called the border patrol. They came and got them."

For a long moment, I don't answer, picturing a mother so desperate to better her life and that of her child that she walked through the heat of the desert, perhaps many hundreds of miles, carrying a nursing infant.

I know what I would have done, whether or not it involved breaking the law. I would have given father, mother, and child food, shelter, and what money we had, and sent them on their way with a blessing.

When I repeat my conversation to Glenn, he sits up straight in his chair, his eyes fierce. "Who is this woman?" he demands. "She needs to be taught a lesson."

I don't tell him. He doesn't need to compound the problem that is, without doubt, one of the major problems facing this part of our country, and one that won't be solved by chastising ignorant neighbors or hiring extra border patrolmen to stem the "invasion."

This is a problem that has its roots in geography, tradition, economics, human nature, and ultimately compassion or its lack.

Yes, I know. I was told by my neighbor that her tax dollars were being handed out to those who run the border to have babies born as U.S. citizens, that she is tired of paying welfare money to ingrates.

But what I know to be true is that there are thousands of men and women who wish to cross our southern border to work, not to be subsidized; to earn an honest living, make enough money to feed themselves, and, in many cases, to be able to return home with cash to take care of entire families.

"Hell! This whole part of the country . . . the ranches, the whole thing, was built by Mexicans," one rancher tells me. "And now when we need workers, we can't hire 'em without a green card, if then."

What he says is correct. Until the Gadsden Purchase, this was Mexico, and the heritage remains in our architecture, music, food, home decoration, in the green chilies I roast and freeze every fall, in the *salsa* that has overtaken American cuisine, in the *vigas* on our houses, the *bosals* with which we train our horses. A look at the map shows the names of valleys and mountains, most of them Spanish — Santa Cruz, Santa Rita, San Pedro, San Simon, and the Animas, Santa Catalina, and Peloncillo ranges. We are using the language and the customs of those here before us while denying them their right to existence.

What disturbs me is the coldness, the ferocity with which one woman, for thoroughly bigoted and selfish reasons, would betray another woman who was nursing an infant.

This incident was compounded by another that occurred while I was shopping in Douglas which, as I tell everyone, might as well be Mexico, a fact that does not bother me in the least. Douglas, with its mixed population and multitude of languages, reminds me of Italy, where I lived for several years, and where human relations make shopping a pleasure, not a chore.

I was going through the checkout at the supermarket when the bagger spoke to me. Since I was busy piling groceries on the moving belt, I didn't hear what she said.

"What?" I asked, and was shocked when she grabbed my arm.

"Forgive me," she said, her eyes sorrowful as a saint's. "Please. I spoke in Spanish. I thought you were Mexican. Please. I'm sorry."

She was an older woman, handsome and intelligent, and I couldn't understand her terror. I laughed. "It's OK. Everybody thinks I'm Mexican. I don't care."

"No!" She held my arm more tightly. "You have to understand that I didn't mean anything. Please. I won't do it again."

Her eyes pleaded, and I was suddenly horrified. The poor woman was frightened out of her wits. Somehow, by speaking to me in Spanish, she had jeopardized herself and her job, in all probability because some bigot had once complained to the management.

Anger is a strange thing. It rises out of blood, bone, a sense of injustice, and what seems to be that forgotten, misplaced feeling labeled "compassion."

I *was* angry. Who, I asked myself, who had so terrorized this nice woman so that she was forced to grovel for my forgiveness? *Who* had rubbed her face in the dirt, threatened her job, her livelihood, simply because she was of another race and country?

Is this what America is all about? Bigotry? Self-righteousness? Terrorism? Is this what my country stands for? Are we, as a nation, going to capture and turn back nursing mothers, men who want to dig ditches, build walls, clean stables, merely to feed themselves? Men ready and willing to work?

Perhaps it is I who has a problem, but I think this is not so. I know a woman who cared for a loyal "illegal," who like his father and grandfather had been working here for a century and who, in his loyalty and haste to return to his job, got caught in a severe mountain blizzard and suffered frostbite.

This woman bathed his feet in warm water and dish soap, nursed him, fed him, listened to his plea that to be sent to the hospital meant being sent home legless and unable to work, swallowed her horror when he, with a knife, cut the dead skin from the soles of his feet. This woman wept — and kept her silence and the man's dignity intact — and rejoiced when he put on his boots and walked out into the yard. Both of them had come through, had survived, because something more than master and servant bound them. Call it respect, friendship, compassion, or even love.

Whatever, I understand the ties that exist, the long-forged bonds between Anglo and Mexican families, between countries that should have no barrier between them but which, instead, have, on our side of the line, a regiment of armed guards and a fearful population.

And I remember that once, many centuries ago, a man, his wife, and their unborn child were not welcome anywhere.

The Bell Jar

East of Douglas the Geronimo Trail narrows and turns from blacktop to a single, rutted lane hemmed by the red rock cones of ancient volcanoes — silent reminders of the origin of these mountains and lava-strewn valleys.

Ahead is the San Bernardino Ranch, once the home of John and Viola Slaughter who left their own indelible mark on the landscape and on history.

Like so many others in the last decades of the 19th Century, the Slaughters were lured here by abundant grass, water, and the freedom that comes with isolation. There were fortunes to be made in the cattle industry and few laws to inhibit the making of those fortunes.

Today the international border cuts the original Slaughter ranch in two, but at the height of his influence John Slaughter's cattle roamed both sides of the line — in those days a fortuitous circumstance which enabled not only Slaughter but many ranchers to enlarge their herds.

We are removed by over a century from the days of the frontier, but as I get out of the car, the years seem to vanish. I am surrounded by ghosts, by the indomitable presence of Slaughter himself; by the quick steps and rippling laughter of Viola, his bride; by the tragedy of Apache May, their adopted Indian child who, playing with fire, burned to death; by the fife and fiddle music of old Bat, devoted servant; and the excited voices of Willie and Addie, Slaughter's children by his first wife.

Glenn and Dan leave me and go off to inspect the house and outbuildings, while I remain in the trance of a time warp, feeling that the entire compound has been encapsulated in a bell jar, preserved in a moment of perfection.

I feel my way into the shadows of history, remember that in 1846 Philip St. George Cook and the Mormon Battalion stopped here on their way to California, and that General Crook used the ruins of an old ranch as base during his war on the Apaches. Once again comes the overwhelming belief that the past can only be brought to life through visual knowledge, and that even the writing of fiction must be based on an understanding of place.

It is midsummer and hot, but there is a

steady breeze from the southwest that stirs the leaves of cottonwoods and white-barked sycamores, makes cat's paws on the surface of the large pond that was the delight of Viola and the ranch children.

For a long time I look into Mexico, an abstraction of striated rock and sand, a shimmer of heat waves dancing over empty desert, a stark landscape at odds with the Slaughter holdings, and which makes obvious the differences between the two countries.

The barb-wire fence marking the border hums in the wind, that tuneless singing one hears in all lonely places in the West. It is the music of empty spaces, of distances too vast to be captured by the eyes.

In moments like this, confirmation of other life becomes necessity, and I walk to the corral where a mare and her foal doze in the shade of the barn. The foal approaches, curious as all young things, sniffs my fingers, watches me out of dark eyes, and I murmur to him and to the mother who nickers, urging caution.

John and Viola Slaughter came to Arizona from New Mexico where John, partly due to the then prevalent practice of "sweeping" all unbranded cattle into his own herd, was Number One on Governor Lew Wallace's

Most Wanted list. It should be noted, however, that, in those years on the frontier, adding unmarked cows to one's own herd was common, and that John Slaughter was certainly not the only cattleman to do so.

He and his young wife ranched for a time in the San Pedro Valley, but in 1884 John purchased the 65,000 acres that became the San Bernardino Ranch.

Those were the years when cattlemen — with an eye for money and the main chance — were forming enormous ranches in Arizona's southeastern valleys. The Chiricahua Cattle Company, The Erie Land and Cattle Company, Hooker's Sierra Bonita, the Babocamari, all became part of the legend of the Western cattle industry, and many, but not all, paid the penalty for overstocking their ranges when struck by the drought of 1892–93.

The lush and nourishing grasses disappeared. In their place came scrub — catclaw, burro weed, tumbleweed, loco — the inedible and sometimes poisonous plants that can, and do, survive when the grass has gone. And much of what we see in these valleys today dates from those years of overgrazing.

Slaughter, however, was more fortunate than most. He had chosen his property with a shrewd eye, noting the many springs and artesian wells, sources of water not only for his range but for that shaded pond east of the house.

Today ducks paddle on the pond's surface. It mirrors sky, immense trees, my face — a white blur that might be any visitor, past or present, lured by shade, water, the happiness of the Slaughter house where visitors were always welcome.

It is a house filled with echoes — as alive today as in the past. The windows are open, curtains move in the breeze, beds are made up, ready for guests, and I turn at the sound of footsteps on the porch, expecting to see Viola, her skirts swirling, her eyes alight.

What I see instead is a boy, his face vacant, his mind in a place I cannot reach. He is playing with a toy — a ball attached by a string to a cup — and he walks past me as if I am not there, or am, perhaps, merely a ghost whom he has seen before. His way is aimless, without destination, like the dust devil that rises suddenly and spins across the yard, and I'm relieved to spot Glenn and Dan coming out of one of the storehouses.

"This place is magic," I say. "It's haunted."

Glenn looks around, takes in the brilliant light, the hush of afternoon, the gauze curtains billowing through tall windows. "Viola was an unusual woman. Why shouldn't she haunt it? Why would she want to be any place else?"

Viola and John lived at the ranch until shortly before John's death in Douglas in 1922. Viola died in 1941, not so long ago that there aren't those who remember her — small and vivacious, riding a big horse in the Fourth of July parades. But Glenn, I think, is right. In her heart she remained here with the man she loved and married over her mother's protest, in the house he built for her. Perhaps she sits unseen on the porch and in the distance watches the coming together of past, present, and future, listens to the whisper of the wind.

Months, years later, I realize that once again a place has been stamped on memory; that its pieces come together as in a puzzle and comprise a whole, so that, peering into the bell jar of remembrance, everything is as it was, even to the foal with its luminous eyes, the saffron and purple distances, the boy who, like me, was attuned to voices making magic in the sunlit air.

Harvest

We have propped up the branches of the apple tree that, for the past ten years, has born bumper crops of a delicious but unknown variety of apple. The magnificent blue and white Talavera pottery bowl that Glenn gave me for Christmas last year is piled to the brim with rosy pomegranates, and a basket on the kitchen counter holds the day's harvest of tomatoes and peppers of all kinds — bell, New Mexico green chilies, Thai hot, and the wild chili tepins, the last two beloved by Dan whose capacity for hot food stuns even fire-eating gourmets.

This is the month when my unceasing labor in the garden receives its reward, and when I go into overdrive canning, baking loaves of zucchini bread to be frozen and brought out for visitors, chopping the ingredients for *salsas* which, in this house, appear in one guise or another at every meal. This is the month that is the joy of gardener and cook, of sensualist and writer.

I revel in the thin skins, juice, and fragrance of just-picked tomatoes, the crispness of peppers, the delicacy of yellow crookneck squash, past its peak but still tender and with a satisfying crunch when chopped in a salad of fresh lettuces, green onions, and tomatoes. I marvel at the diversity of edible plants, both in taste and beauty.

Nothing is lovelier than an eggplant — purple, globular, warm from the sun, and nestling in my hand. I remember the fragrance of my grandmother's kitchen — her eggplant *parmigiana,* her thick and delicious sauces, and how always, on one deep window sill, she kept a rosemary plant and a red geranium, and where an orange cat seemed always to be sleeping, its paws tucked under, its eyes green slits.

Last week Diane Freund told me the superstition that as long as one has an orange cat, one will prosper. This is new to me, but I believe it, for my grandmother always had an orange cat, and more than enough to feed her family and friends who dropped in to spend an hour talking, drinking coffee, and sampling the delicacies that came from her oven.

Outside her kitchen door was a grape arbor that, in late summer and fall, produced grapes that could have graced a Dutch still life. Beyond that was my grandfather's garden, a fantasy I have tried to replicate without success. My grand-father grew everything from corn to kohlrabi, every day bringing baskets of produce to pile on the long pine table that served both as eating place and altar where food was prepared.

This, I tell myself, is part of me — blood, bone, genetic thrust. I am a planter — of seeds and words — and both develop with proper nurturing. I am a woman who revels in mixtures of colors and tastes, in the growing of herbs and the use of them to enhance, in the satisfaction that comes from seeing those at my table eat to repletion.

And had I been born a rancher, the same pleasure would have been derived from nurturing my pastures. This discovery came tonight when Glenn and I walked out to check the grass that has grown ungrazed for several summers.

Thirteen years ago there was barely enough forage to support one cow, let alone our original two horses. Now, after planned pasture rotation, good fencing, and several fine rainy seasons, the grass is as it was once — hip high and lush — a mixture of grama, timothy, galleta, lovegrass, and others I can't name.

Once again I hear Archie saying: "Time

was . . . the grama was high as a man's stirrups . . . so thick the snakes rode on the top. . . ."

I wish Archie could see our pastures. I wish he could walk with us on grass so thick our feet don't touch the soil, on a golden carpet cured on the stem and bending down with seeds to secure the next generation.

I wish those ranchers of a century ago could see what a small amount of management and foresight and a great deal of Glenn's expertise and labor have achieved — a sea of grass, acres of it — with a full moon slipping above the mountains, smiling like a blessing.

And I wish my grandmother could come into my kitchen where the rich fragrance of tomato sauce scents the air. I think she would approve in her solemn way. I think she would sit down, sample the pasta, the meatballs, the *bracciole* made as I remember she made it, and smile like the moon, and say: *"Qui, si mangia bene."*

Who could ask for more?

Sunglow Again

The invitation to the open house came in the mail. Sunglow had been bought, refurbished, and was to be a guest ranch again.

I had been back only once — when it stood forlorn and empty in the cup of its small valley. Seeing it silent, the corrals empty, and with the knowledge that the horses had all been sent to the killers without regard either for their value or their being opened a wound that had taken a long time to heal.

After that visit I never returned, but the invitation changed things. Obviously someone cared for the place and had brought it back to the life it deserved.

Dan went with me on a stained-glass afternoon in mid-October. We took the back way through Rucker Cañon, past the ruins of the old Army fort, and through the Chiricahuas where the cottonwoods spilled yellow leaves into sun-struck air, and every turn of the road reminded us of another, earlier time.

Red earth, black globes of juniper, bunch

grass, chamiso, the almost hidden turn-off to Edith's house, and, like a painted backdrop, the mass of the mountains, a permanent force, a repository of hope and dreams.

Twenty years before I had come here as a stranger, a woman lost and searching for identity and the route to the words locked inside. Twenty years! They seemed only a heartbeat. So it came as a shock to be introduced as an old-timer, someone who remembered Sunglow as it had been, who'd known Archie and Edith, Woodie, Al, and Jeanne, as a writer whose first books were set here, inspired by the echoes of history, the sorrow and joy of those whose stories I had made my own — Archie's mother who lost her newborn when an illiterate midwife washed it by mistake in carbolic acid; Grandma Price and her brood; Susannah who married the wrong man but learned to love him; and the outlaw, John Ringo, whose grave is just over the hill on the banks of Turkey Creek.

It is strange that even now, over a hundred years later, the fact of his killing is still being argued, the events rehashed, when it has been proved that Ringo was killed by Wyatt Earp who, set on vengeance for the murder of his brother Morgan, secretly returned from Colorado with Doc Holliday and tracked his prey to the lonely cañon that bisects the road to Morse's Sawmill and the outlaw hang-out, Galeyville.

"Nowadays, folks come in here and think they know everything, but they don't." I can recall Archie's words, spoken with more than a hint of scorn for those he knows as history fakers.

"My dad knew the truth of it. We all did. Ringo was shot some place else and stuck in that tree so somebody would be sure to find him. They all knew who did it, too, but back then we minded our own business. What was done was done."

And what was done has become part of the on-going myth of the Earp legend.

Earth spins, mountains are touched by sunlight and shadow, the past exists simultaneously with the now. It has always been so.

And on that afternoon at Sunglow, when Jeanne and Al stepped out of their car and stood smiling, time became meaningless. I was running into the past in a repetition of an act done many times before, and I was laughing because, by a miracle, I had come full circle.

Billy

Our friend Max is sitting in the living room scowling. He has finished reading *Moving On*, my collection of short fiction that he says he loves with one exception.

"I can't see how you could write '*Corrido for Billy*'," he says. "No matter what, you'll never convince me that Billy the Kid was anything but the scum of the earth!"

Glenn and I look at each other, well aware of the pros and cons of the Lincoln County War and Billy's rôle in it, and we both remember when, to our dismay, a *Newsweek* reporter likened the Kid to "Charles Manson in cowboy boots."

With a provocative gleam in his eye, Glenn asks: "How much have you read about Lincoln County history?"

"Not that much," Max admits. "But it doesn't take brains to know the Kid was a no-good juvenile delinquent!"

"You've seen too many movies," Glenn tells him. "Hollywood always gets it wrong. I'll give you some books, and then you should go look at Billy the Kid country. It'll give you a feel for what was going on at the time."

Max laughs. "I'll read the books, but I don't give a damn about scenery."

But it is in the land that the truth is hidden. It is in the mountains, valleys, and endless plains of New Mexico that the legend of the Kid comes to life.

I have ridden down the valley of the Hondo in spring when the apple trees were blooming and their petals showered me with pink light. With Glenn, I have explored Lincoln in the heat of summer, seen it buried in November snow, wandered through Tularosa in the shadow of Sierra Blanca. Together we have followed Route 70 east out of Ruidoso past the marker recording the death of John Tunstall, past the ranch that was once the home of the infamous Harrell brothers, and which now belongs to the family of artists Peter Hurd and Henriette Wyeth, through old San Patricio where Billy gambled at monte.

The road twists, turns, descends, and rises again, and then, without warning, teeters above the sweep of the High Plains — an immensity of shapes and colors — blue, olive, the pale dun of wild horses, the purple of cloud shadow — a chord of music that vibrates down my spine.

No matter how often we have taken this journey, the visual impact of place always leaves me light-headed with longing. But for what?

There are times when, standing at the edge of the plains, I think I would like to be turned to stone, to become an inseparable part of indomitable and vibrant space — a curved shape pressed into the prairie and gradually turning to dust. This is not a wish for death but for eternal life, a caring beyond all caring for the double-edged blade of what is, in itself, perfection.

Like Frederick Jackson Turner, I believe that the land marks us, that what we do or become is often in reaction to environment. The protagonists of the Lincoln County War, Billy included, played out rôles that had been in part written by geography. The rest of the script was dictated by human nature in all its complexity, a tangled skein of events motivated by love, loyalty, passion, and, most of all, by greed.

At one time I had planned to do a novel on Lincoln County, but, in the course of my research, discovered that I had more questions than answers and a multitude of characters, weak and strong, good and evil that would take me years to comprehend.

But what I knew intuitively was that in the

rugged, changeable landscape of New Mexico the Kid had found his place of belonging. He rode it, understood it and its people — those he loved and was loyal to, and those he hated — in his bones. And his feelings were reciprocated. It was not by chance that honest ranchers like the Coes and the English gentleman, Tunstall, respected him, and that the Mexican population protected him and gave him shelter. Like him, they saw the truth, saw the hunger for power, the political machinations that, as always in history, were the underlying cause of violence and war. And, as always, they recognized an honest heart.

I do not say any of this to Max because he will not be convinced. Like so many others, he has seized upon the image of the Kid as a peyote-gobbling, snarling street kid, a product of Hollywood and the 20th Century and not of an earlier, far different and much misunderstood era.

He has read my story, read that the Mexican women who prepared Billy for burial after he was murdered by Pat Garrett remembered another Billy. He was their *"chivito,"* their "little ram," an angry boy set on revenge for the killing of his friend John Tunstall, a man who could not bring himself to leave the people or the country that he loved, not even to save himself.

For Max, and for others, this will not be proof enough, but no matter. What I wrote was what the mountains told me, and the plains. I wrote a love story about a poignant moment at Pete Maxwell's house in old Fort Sumner one long ago night in the year 1881.

Vaya con Dios, Billy.

Epilogue

It has been an unusually rainy fall. From the Interstate, the Animas Playa appears like a mirage, a miles-long stretch of blue water where, a month ago were only sand, scrub, waves of heat and spiraling dust devils.

The cranes have returned, and at the edge of a still pool, a snowy egret, flash of brilliant white, stands motionless above its reflection.

Once hunted almost to extinction for their plumage like the whooping cranes, the snowy egret has made a gradual comeback, although the sight of one is always memorable.

Last year I came upon two of them in a mesquite beside our pond. It is hard to say which of us was the more startled, the birds that, frightened by my approach, shattered the air with sudden flight, or me, shielding my eyes from the blaze of white wings against dark blue sky.

I have tried many times since to capture that moment in a poem, and have always failed, perhaps because the impressions are too many and too vivid, the purity of colors — pure white, deep blue, the red ochre of mountains — magnified in recollection. Or perhaps the Muse has not come with the precise words. Not yet.

To one unaccustomed to the high desert, this landscape of rock, sand, and occasional water must seem barren, devoid of beauty, but to me, driving home after a five-day book tour, each sculpted hill, each cloud formation is not only a welcome, but an image perfect in conception and existing in no other place.

On this day, the playa mirrors the sky, and I note with the satisfaction of familiarity that, as happens every autumn, the mountains seem to have receded into themselves, an illusory transformation brought about by the slant of the sun, a gentling of summer's bold definition and sharp shadow.

The colors now are pastels — dun, rose, the pale olive of cured grasses, with here and there, on the curving slopes, the dark thrust of a juniper, the bronze of creosote.

I leave the Interstate and the playa behind, slow for an instant at the top of Granite Gap. Below, the San Simon Valley is a study in gold, the composition of an Impressionist, its distance blurred by a faint haze that shivers in the still air.

This is my valley, this sweep of yellow earth held between mountains, this still sparsely populated place of silence and bird song, wind and solitude.

More than fifteen years have passed since I closed the door on one life and entered another, not without fear, but armed with the fragile belief that I was more than a cowering wife, and that the voice within deserved its chance.

Perhaps even more important, I was a woman who had never been allowed to love another without some form of reprisal. Was it a miracle that I came here, to the place where I belong, to the man I loved and married?

Although I believe in destiny, I also believe that destiny belongs to the self, that we can either make choices and change or ignore the voices that urge us on; that we can permit the erasure of all that we are or fight for the right to realize our potential.

From here I cannot see the house, only the cliffs and cañons of the Chiricahuas, the rounded domes of the Peloncillos, but I know that Glenn is there waiting. And I know that somewhere to the south and east is the volcanic hill that I photographed for the cover of one of my books which, I've been told, is now known locally as "Jane's Mountain."

I think of Juan de Oñate's inscription carved into rock. The words *"Pasó por aquí,"* and his name are all that remain of the Spanish expedition that marched through these valleys searching for gold and the Seven Cities of Cibola. There were, of course, no such cities. They existed only in the dreams of the potential conquerors.

But what they found contained different riches. Here were mountains, rivers, plains, sky, the silence of untouched places. Here was a land that touched the heart, a country beyond imagination, often beyond description. What they found was my place of belonging, where on the red slopes of Jane's Mountain the poppies fire the grass in spring, and in autumn one cottonwood glimmers in the long rays of afternoons.

And so I write on this page in hope of leaving my own hymn to life, love, these long and lonely valleys.

"Pasó por aquí."

Cochise County, Arizona,
near Rodeo, New Mexico
November, 2000
Jane Candia Coleman

About the Author

Born and raised near Pittsburgh, Pennsylvania, Jane Candia Coleman majored in creative writing at the University of Pittsburgh but stopped writing after graduation in 1960 because she knew she "hadn't lived enough, thought enough, to write anything of interest." Her life changed dramatically when she abandoned the East for the West in 1986, and her creativity came truly into its own. *The Voices of Doves* (1988) was written soon after she moved to Tucson. It was followed by a book of poetry, *No Roof but Sky* (1990), and by a truly remarkable short story collection that amply repays reading and re-reading, *Stories from Mesa Country* (1991). Her short story, "Lou" in *Louis L'Amour Western Magazine* (3/94), won the Spur Award from the Western Writers of America as did her later short story, "Are You Coming Back, Phin Montana?" in *Louis L'Amour Magazine* (1/96). She has also won three Western Heritage Awards from the National Cowboy Hall of Fame. *Doc Holliday's Woman* (1995) was her first novel and one of vivid and extraordinary power. The highly acclaimed *Moving On: Stories of the West* was her first **Five Star Western,** and it contains her two Spur award-winning stories. It was followed in 1998 with the novel, *I, Pearl Hart.* It can be said that a story by Jane Candia Coleman embodies the essence of what is finest in the Western story, intimations of hope, vulnerability, and courage, while she plummets to the depths of her characters, conjuring moods and imagery with the consummate artistry of an accomplished poet.